read
and send
the right
signals

A PRACTICAL GUIDE TO BODY LANGUAGE

GLENN WILSON

This edition published in the UK
in 2018 by Icon Books Ltd,
Omnibus Business Centre,
39–41 North Road,
London N7 9DP
email: info@iconbooks.com
www.iconbooks.com

First published in the UK
in 2012 by Icon Books

Sold in the UK, Europe and Asia
by Faber & Faber Ltd,
Bloomsbury House,
74–77 Great Russell Street,
London WC1B 3DA
or their agents

Distributed in South Africa
by Jonathan Ball,
Office B4, The District,
41 Sir Lowry Road,
Woodstock 7925

Distributed in Australia and
New Zealand
by Allen & Unwin Pty Ltd,
PO Box 8500,
83 Alexander Street,
Crows Nest,
NSW 2065

Distributed in Canada
by Publishers Group Canada,
76 Stafford Street, Unit 300
Toronto,
Ontario M6J 2S1

Distributed in the USA
by Publishers Group West,
1700 Fourth Street,
Berkeley, CA 94710

ISBN: 978-178578-388-3

Typeset in Avenir by Marie Doherty

Printed and bound in Great Britain by Clays Ltd, Elcograf S.p.A.

About the author

Dr Glenn Wilson is a Consultant Psychologist in London and a Fellow of the British Psychological Society. Previously he was a Visiting Professor of Psychology at Gresham College, London and a Professor at the University of Nevada, Reno. He specialises in personality, interpersonal attraction and reading body language.

Contents

sides to the face. Flushing and blushing. The importance of gaze.

How to tell whether other people are on-side or interested in us. Are they warm or cold, attracted or repulsed? Reading the signals of courtship and intimacy. Recognising when someone is bored with us. How to make someone warm towards us.

How can we tell if someone is sincere or being deceitful? Some famous liars and how they might have been spotted. How to come across as trustworthy. New technologies for lie detection.

When do we feel 'crowded'? Etiquette concerning the use of space. Jostling for territory. The sun lounger syndrome. Body orientation and seating arrangements. How space can be manipulated to make us seem powerful or to put others at their ease.

How the power game is played out in the ordinary world and among politicians. The signals of dominance and submission. Handshakes and their meaning. Bodily stance. Strategies for getting what we want.

The evolutionary basis of beauty and sex appeal. Signals of masculinity/femininity. Innate releasers and imprinting of sex targets. How to tell if someone is unattached and attracted to us. Body language at parties. Techniques of flirting. Proteans and pseudo-flirting. The meaning of kisses. Tone of voice. Tips for impressing women and seducing men.

What is stress and what are the signs? How do we know when someone is under pressure and about to crack emotionally? How do we detect rising stress in ourselves? What can we do to relax and take control when we detect that our own stress levels are rising out of control? Stressed relationships.

Body language on the stage. How actors convey feelings through the use of posture and gesture. Do they need to experience these feelings themselves or can they be generated in an audience through technique alone? Can charisma be acquired? How to make a good speech.

1. Everybody's second language

Fie, fie upon her!
There's language in her eye, her cheek, her lip.
Nay, her foot speaks: her wanton spirits look out
At every joint and motive of her body.

Ulysses, in Shakespeare's *Troilus and Cressida*

I speak two languages – Body and English.

Mae West

There are many jokes about dogs that talk. They are funny because we know that dogs don't talk. Or do they? Dog owners know that Fido can express himself quite effectively in a variety of ways. He can wag his tail and bark excitedly when anticipating food or walkies. He can lower his head and cower as though expecting to be hit when feeling guilty about stealing some sausages. These emotions are readily understood by dog owners. Fido can also glean a great deal about how we are disposed towards him from our gestures and behaviour. Although he might be responsive to the shape of certain words, such as his own name, most of this communication is through the reading of body language and tone of voice.

Humans don't have to rely on such indirect signals because we have an advanced language capability and can state our case much more clearly and explicitly. At least we think we can.

All of the emotional signalling that animals use is still present in humans and registers importantly with us. After all, we cannot always trust what someone tells us: they may have reasons for wanting to be deceptive. Some things, like cold facts and statistics, are best communicated by words and numbers – but attitudes and intentions are better read through body language.

In some ways, body language is even more highly developed in humans because we have a most expressive face that has developed in connection with our preferred front-on interaction. Powerful signals are transmitted by facial expressions. We also have a highly developed capacity for 'mind-reading'. This is the very useful capacity to second-guess what somebody has 'in mind' for us based on voice inflexions and body language cues. Obviously it is important to know whether or not someone fancies us or wishes we would just go away. It is important to know whether they are on-side or on the verge of attack. Mind-reading ability has been retained and in some ways further evolved in humans because it has considerable survival value.

Where there is a discrepancy between what is said verbally and the feelings that are indirectly transmitted through facial expression and body language, we quite rightly set greater store by what we see, rather than what we are being told. This is because body language 'leaks' certain emotions and attitudes that we might have preferred to conceal from those who observe us (and they know it). The reception process is immediate and largely unconscious, though it can be made conscious through a process of analysis such as that used in this book.

It is widely said that 93% of our communication is through body language, while only 7% is based in the words themselves. Although Albert Mehrabian, the researcher on whose work in the 1960s this assertion is based, has said this is a simplification of his findings, others have produced data suggesting that around 60–70% of our communication is non-verbal.

CASE STUDY Studies of US presidential election campaigns have been done in which the speeches of candidates are assessed through watching videos with and without sound, listening to sound recordings alone and simply reading transcripts. This allows comparison of the power of the various channels to influence voter choices and it confirms that visual body language, and even tone of voice, are much more persuasive than the verbal content of the message. Not surprisingly a new breed of 'spin doctors', image consultants and television coaches has grown in strength.

It is now widely recognised that what we often think of as our second language is actually of more importance than our first. Any poker player, salesperson, investigating detective, actor or nightclub dancer will attest to this, so it is important to study it and understand its principles.

Seen and not heard

Next time you are at a noisy cocktail party or social function where you can barely hear the person you are talking to, take a look at groups of people interacting across the other side of the room. Even though you cannot hear a word they say, you will be able to divine a great deal about what is really going on between them and their true feelings and intentions towards each other. Perhaps one is making a play for the other that you can tell is unwelcome and will come to nothing. One may be clearly dominant over the others because the others are all respectful and attentive towards that individual. In a funny way, you can often tell *more* about the real relationships among people when you are not distracted by the content of the 'small talk' that is going on between them.

But how can you ever know if you were right? The same effect can be achieved by turning off the sound on the TV when a drama or soap is playing. An amusing party game is to supply some of the dialogue that you cannot hear on a video, then afterwards replay it with the sound up to see how far wide of the mark you were. At the very least, you will probably have been right about which characters were at loggerheads and which were enjoying warm rapport. If you were wrong, was it bad acting, or was there some additional agenda or undercurrent that might explain why the words were inconsistent with the body language?

Deaf people are particularly good at the body language game (even without lip-reading) because they have more experience at the skill. The American performance artist Terry Galloway, author of the book *Mean, Little, Deaf, Queer* (2009), reported on her own experience of going deaf in early childhood as a side-effect of an antibiotic: 'Deafness has left me acutely aware of both the duplicity that language is capable of and the many expressions the body cannot hide.' There is also some evidence that women are better at reading body language than men, which is the truth in the phrase 'women's intuition'.

The beast within

What is the origin of this non-verbal code to which we are all responsive? The great evolutionary biologist Charles Darwin pointed out that the expression of an emotion is usually achieved by delivering a sample or residue of a more complete and overt instinctive behavioural pattern.

'Disgust' literally means rejecting something that is foul tasting. Even though it may be induced by social events, the facial expression of disgust still resembles regurgitation of tainted food. Fear is indicated in various ways: by freezing, by preparing to flee or by clinging hold of someone/something for support. Such strategies might be of value when confronted with a lion in the wild but they are less appropriate when the source of 'danger' is an audience to whom we have to make a speech. This is why 'stage fright' is something we try to overcome.

A dog snarls in anger as a threat to bite. In much the same way, when humans are angry they show preparation to fight. They clench their teeth, make a fist with their hand and thrust their head forward. They may not actually be about to bite, punch or butt the other person but they are indicating that they are inclined to. Body language enables us to make threats to others that, if properly received and responded to, can deflect actual aggression. In this way competitor males do not necessarily have to fight to the death to establish dominance. A ritual struggle will do instead. Of course, it doesn't always work: sometimes the mere act of looking at another person is seen as aggressive and violence is provoked, especially among testosterone-fuelled young male gangs. But for much of human interaction a show of anger may be sufficient without the need for actual violence.

When a cat wants to show trust it rolls over on its back and exposes its belly, inviting us to tickle it. When a woman is feeling sexually receptive towards someone she will expose vulnerable areas of the body such as the wrists and neck – the parts that are normally well protected. We may not be aware of the exact significance of each gesture but the overall impression is usually quite accurate. Body language can be used as an invitation to greater intimacy without the need for showing cards upwards on the table, and the invitation can be subtly declined without major loss of face.

Cross-cultural accord

Many emotional expressions are universal across cultures. For example, people throughout the world smile and laugh when happy, and they cry or frown when sad. In all places, the 'eyebrow flash' (lifting the eyebrows in pleasant surprise) is used when greeting an old friend that one has not seen in a long time. Even monkeys do this, confirming the evolution of our body language. Turning the head from side to side means 'no' in any culture and anthropologists trace this to the suckling baby turning its head away from its mother's breast when it has had enough milk.

The tendency of women to make brief eye contact with a man and then avert their gaze away and downward is observed even in little girls born blind. This means that it could not have been acquired through imitation. While we might think of it as a display of female modesty, some anthropologists interpret this behaviour as a ritual invitation to chase, the expectation being that they would eventually be run down and caught by a 'fit' male. This is why gaze-averting comes across as a flirtatious gesture. The courting male would thus be tested both for his determination and his physical fitness, attributes that would be useful in any offspring that might result from mating with him. Whatever the precise interpretation, the appearance of universal behavioural patterns of this kind may be taken as evidence of their instinctual origin.

Conveying refusal

Ask a friend to role-play an actor doing an audition. Their job is to say the line: 'No, I absolutely will not do what you ask' direct to the camera. If you have a mobile phone that will record a video of them doing this, all the better. Almost certainly, they will be seen to turn their head from side to side in support of the verbal refusal. This is a cross-culturally universal gesture that probably derives from the infant's turning away from the mother's breast when satiated.

Failure of mind-reading skills

For the majority of people, the capacity for reading body language emerges spontaneously at a certain age. However, for a minority (mostly males) the mind-reading module in the brain seems to be largely absent and social skills are mastered only with difficulty or not at all. Such individuals are called autistic, or described as suffering from

Asperger's Syndrome, because they lack the ability to connect properly and empathise with others.

Since this deficit is based in early (even pre-natal) brain development, with no obvious differences in upbringing, it appears that the reading of body language is a natural human function. The same is true for verbal language: although the environment determines which particular language we speak, the development of the grammatical and other deep structures of language unfolds quite spontaneously. And here too, the process is more reliable in female than male children.

Posture and gesture

There is a distinction to be made between posture and gesture that is crucial to the reading of body language.

A *gesture* is a socially learned signal that involves only one part of the body (usually the hand). It tends to be disconnected from the rest of the body and is usually devoid of emotional investment. When we are asked a street direction by a stranger we casually point the way with our finger, while the rest of our body is not involved. Pointing to the side of one's head to indicate that someone is lacking in the brains department is another example of a hand gesture that does not go beyond the hand and which depends upon the observers agreeing on its meaning.

Gestural codes differ from place to place and there is great scope for misunderstanding. Making a small circle between the forefinger and thumb has many different meanings around the world: in some places it means 'zero' or 'worthless', in Japan it means money, but in Italy it means homosexual. Jerking the thumb upwards means 'OK' in English-speaking countries and is used by hitchhikers to solicit a ride. In Greece it is an obscene insult roughly equivalent to 'get stuffed', hence the lack of success experienced there by some British hitchhikers.

 Such misunderstandings may have fatal consequences. Two holidaymaking swimmers who had strayed from Greek waters into Albania were shot dead because they mistook a beckoning signal from the border guards as telling them to go away. Around this part of Europe there is a point where the beckon gesture changes from 'pulling' with palms upward to waving the hands forward and downward. It can be very important to know the code.

A *posture* involves the whole of the body acting in concert. This is usually invested with much greater emotional significance and conveys deep feelings. If, rather than pointing out a street direction, we are pointing to a child who is about to be hit by a bus, the whole of our body will be aligned so as to communicate the urgency of the situation. This shows a consistent, instinctive attitude, rather than an empty signal that may be culturally variable. It is one of the ways in which we are able to assess the feelings and intentions of others.

Part of the art of reading body language is therefore to look past gestures and evaluate postures.

 Most of the points above will be illustrated more clearly as we go through the book. However, it is worth summarising some major principles at the outset:

1. Body language is rooted in our animal past. It is largely transmitted and read unconsciously. It can be subsequently broken down and analysed but the registration is more immediate than that. It is processed by brain modules that have evolved because they aid survival.

2. Where body language conflicts with the words that are being said, the body language will usually be the more 'truthful' in the sense of revealing true feelings.

3. Where body language is giving mixed signals (e.g. a smile that borders on a grimace or fails to involve the eyes) then the more negative, less socially desirable component is usually the more telling. This is because we are more often motivated to conceal unpleasant truths and anti-social feelings than pleasant, benign ones.

4. Where there is a discrepancy between a particular hand gesture and the rest of the body (a posture), the posture will be the more telling.

The many applications

In the pages of this book we show how the management of our own body language and the reading of that in others has important relevance to our social survival in many real-life contexts. These include such areas as:

1. Conducting ourselves in a job interview or evaluating a candidate for a job.

2. Attracting a partner in a singles bar or party and spotting whether a potential partner fancies us.

3. Assessing the warmth and sincerity of current partners, friends or strangers.

4. Interrogating a suspect at a police station or in a courtroom.

5. Recognising when road rage is potentially dangerous.

6. Spotting whether or not a salesperson is being deceitful.

7. Learning to be an effective actor or performer.

8. Delivering a persuasive speech at a conference or making a favourable impression in a TV interview.

In almost any aspect of our social lives, the ability to interpret accurately the signals of body language, and to manage the impression we are giving to others, may be critical to our success, or even our survival.

CASE STUDY

The demise of Captain Cook

Captain James Cook, the great English explorer and cartographer, met his death in Hawaii in 1779, and a failure of body language may have been responsible. In one account, he stuck out his hand to shake with the islanders' chief in a typically British act of greeting that was misread as an aggressive gesture, resulting in him being speared to death on the beach. In another account, which perhaps has more credibility, he was first received as a god by the islanders and given both deference and provisions. However, shortly after setting sail, his ship was ravaged by a storm, the mainmast was snapped, and he had to return for repairs. This enabled the witchdoctors (who were envious of his status and felt displaced) to denounce him as a fraud. Thus stripped of his aura of invincibility, he became involved in violent skirmishes with the islanders and was ultimately pursued and killed as he and his crew attempted to return to the stricken ship. Either way, this example shows how a command of body language and its cultural variations may literally be a matter of life and death.

2. How do I look?

We are often told not to judge a book by its cover. Yet that is precisely what we do a lot of the time. We sum up others at a glance by the way they are dressed and presented and by certain aspects of their body language and facial expression. Are they clean and well-groomed? Is their dress appropriate for the situation? Do they move with a confident gait? Do they smile warmly and make eye contact? It is as though we take an immediate snapshot of a person that is almost indelible and which determines our reaction to them. We might revise our opinion after we hear how they speak, learn what they have to say and what finer personality traits and other virtues they have to offer. But only with great reluctance do we change a negative evaluation based on that initial glance. The first impression sets the stage for all further interaction.

When people are shown photographs of strangers' faces whose personality has been previously assessed, they are able to detect immediately those who are high in 'psychoticism'. This is a major personality trait that is partly inherited and which goes with slightly weird behaviour, irresponsibility, risk-taking, criminal activity and delinquency. Quite how we are able to judge this in the faces of others is a bit of a mystery because the facial differences were not obvious to the researchers. However, there are clear survival advantages in spotting someone untrustworthy, especially for a woman choosing a partner. No such ability to detect other personality traits such as extraversion or neuroticism from facial characteristics alone has been found, but there are many other cues we can pick up on.

Gaining an impression

When you are sitting in a park or on a bus and feel like playing a little game, try the following. Pick out a particular individual that you have never met and glance at them for a couple of seconds. Now close your eyes and go through some questions in your head.

1. How old are they?
2. What is their nationality and ethnic group?
3. What is their social class?
4. What job do they do (if any)?
5. Where are they going and what are they involved in doing at present?
6. What is their personality like? Are they friendly or cold, trustworthy or unreliable, aggressive or timid?
7. How well do you think you would get on with them socially?

It doesn't matter whether you are right or wrong (you will probably never find out) but it is interesting to note that you probably believe you can make these sort of judgements after only a brief glance. So what cues are you working on?

The reason we can assess people so rapidly is that we compare what we see before us with a set of previously established *stereotypes* – expectations based on what we have been told and what we have gained from past experience. Usually there is some element of truth in these stereotypes but they can also be misleading.

 Getting it wrong
An episode in a British courtroom some years ago illustrates how seriously misleading stereotypes can be. A young black lawyer with dreadlocks was escorting his client, a white man in a suit, into the courtroom at his trial. The usher directed the lawyer towards the prisoner's dock on the presumption that he was the one who was charged. This resulted in great embarrassment all round. Clearly, the usher had seen many men with dreadlocks in the dock but he had never previously encountered one who was a lawyer.

Obviously, people should be free to present themselves any way they like, but they need to be aware that every choice has consequences with respect to how they are perceived. Young men who hang around street corners wearing hoodies and gloves on a warm night are picked out disproportionately for 'stop and search' by the police. Criminals, drug dealers and gang members have uniforms every bit as much as soldiers and police officers, even though 'uniforms' like hoodies and gloves might be shared by other, entirely innocent social groups.

The way women dress can transmit signals regarding their sexual interest and availability, which will often affect the likelihood of their receiving sexual advances. It's worth noting that scanty clothing, or what we might think of as dressing provocatively, doesn't mean that all sexual advances will be welcome, and interested parties still bear responsibility for how they interpret and act on the perceived signals sent by clothing and body language. At the other end of the clothing spectrum is the concealment favoured by nuns and some Islamic groups, which critics claim is an insult to men because it implies they would not otherwise be able to contain their bestial urges. We all have choices to make about how we present ourselves to others but we need to be aware of their likely impact, as well as being conscientious in how we interpret the choices others make.

Clothes maketh the man (and woman)

What can we tell about a person by the way they dress? For one thing, we might get clues as to how much money they have to spend. It also gives away much about how they want to be seen by others – the image that they choose to project. One can spend a lot on clothes yet still not appear as ostentatious. Designer labels do not have to be vaunted by massive letters that are intended to impress others. Expensive fabrics may be evident simply by the way they are tailored and hang on the body without any need for trumpeting.

Regardless of expense, the way we are dressed can show how much pride we take in ourselves and how we value cleanliness. The impression given can range from careless and sloppy to precious and obsessional. Perhaps the most important thing is to be appropriate; we are generally most comfortable when wearing the right thing for the occasion. The man who wears a suit at the beach looks slightly ridiculous, as does the man who wears trainers with a dinner jacket and bow tie.

Broadly speaking, men dress to display status. They use their clothes as a kind of uniform or badge of identity. Many men still wear a tie as a symbol of occupational status or respectability. However, showing freedom from the necessity of being 'bonded' in this way may be an even greater statement of social power. Top actors like Colin Firth and businessmen like Richard Branson feel no need to 'conform' in this way. A bow tie comes across as slightly arty and eccentric, if possibly a bit affected. Choice of colour may also be telling: research suggests that ambitious men and introverts favour discreet colours like grey, blue and brown, while extraverts and thrill-seekers go for brighter colours like red and orange.

Women also often dress to display status, particularly those who hold positions of power. They may be sending signals to other women or colleagues concerning their wealth and social position, or that of their partner.

Expensive jewellery, hairstyles, hats and blatantly displayed designer labels help them to do this. Women may also dress to enhance sexual signals or dampen them down, depending on their interest at the time.

 Psychoanalyst J.C. Flugel introduced the concept of **power dressing** as early as 1930. His idea was that people who wanted to get ahead in the world should dress for dominance, with large shoulder pads, vertical stripes to increase apparent height, and sharp, pointy, 'masculine' lines to their clothes. Whereas women's clothes were traditionally soft, rounded, pink and fluffy (in line with their passive role and skin texture), men's clothes were supposed to reflect their active, thrusting role, being hard-edged and angular. For Flugel, the black brolly, tails, bowler hat, blade-shaped tie and lapels and shiny black shoes were all to some degree phallic symbols. Certainly, they could be regarded as the antithesis of feminine softness.

This theory helps to explain why polishing boots is such an important military ritual and why mediaeval authorities condemned pointed-toe shoes as lecherous and provocative. A fifteenth-century Papal Bull described the *poulaine* (upturned shoe) as 'scoffing against God and the Church'. Likewise, during the reign of Edward IV, it was decreed that 'no knight under the rank of a lord … shall wear shoes or boots having pikes or points exceeding the length of two inches, under forfeiture of forty pence'. The concern was that people should know their place and reflect it properly in their style of dress.

As women moved into occupations that were once male-dominated they also had to engage in power dressing in order to compete (recall the monstrous lapels worn by women in American soaps of the 1970s and 80s like *Dallas* and *Dynasty*). Remnants of this persist today in that women in executive positions often wear pinstriped suits and shorter haircuts on the presumption that appearing more masculine will increase their credibility in the workplace.

THINK ABOUT IT

What do a person's shoes tell you?
Imagine that you can see only the shoes someone is wearing. What do you think you might be able to infer from that? Many people – men in particular – think their shoes are unimportant because they are below the usual gaze line. This is quite mistaken. Shoes are boundary markers and thus stand out with greater significance. We talk about people being 'down at heel', 'well shod' or 'on their uppers', alerting us to the fact that shoe style and condition is a key marker of economic status and prestige. Shoes are often a giveaway of the type of occupation one has. For doctors, lawyers and salespeople, clean, shiny shoes are virtually essential, whereas for other jobs (farmer or decorator) cleaning one's

21

shoes would be a waste of time. This is why clean shoes are seen as important by employers and clients: the person who does not bother to clean their shoes is subconsciously relegated to the class for whom shoe-cleaning is futile. Far from going unnoticed, shoes are major indicators of grooming, on a par with clean hair and teeth.

What sort of car?

Just as the male bower bird has replaced the cumbersome tail display of the peacock in favour of elaborate colourful constructions that draw attention to their fitness, so modern men display status indirectly in a number of ways. One of the best known is the kind of car that a man drives.

Research shows that women do judge status (hence desirability) by the car men drive. Luxury cars such as a Bentley, Mercedes, Audi or Lexus convey high status. Large four-by-fours like Land Rovers can be impressive but suggest a more practical attitude, and high-wheeled cars are often driven by women because they feel more secure. Hatchbacks imply a family man/woman and the drivers of sports cars are likely to come across as desperate to impress. When a woman drives a sports car it is perceived as a slightly aggressive show of independence and can be intimidating. 'Mondeo Man' is a way of dubbing the ordinary person, while the image of 'white van man' is so well known as to require no comment.

Hairstyles

The courtroom example on page 17 illustrates how important hairstyles may be. Long hair on a woman is associated with femininity and youth, which is why Muslim women are often required to cover their hair in public, for reasons of modesty. Short hair often suggests a businesslike attitude or greater maturity, and is often adopted by women in positions of power, such as Angela Merkel or Hillary Rodham Clinton. In men, excessively long hair looks bohemian and may create a tramp-like impression if it is not properly washed and styled. Very short hair sometimes comes across as thuggish (the 'skinhead' look) but is fashionable among certain groups and those who are making the best of encroaching baldness. Outlandish hair colours like green and magenta, and styles like the Mohican, also carry a message – usually non-conformity and eccentricity. However, no hard and fast rules can be laid down because the acceptability of various hairstyles is context-dependent and subject to rapid social change.

THINK ABOUT IT

Blonde or brunette?

If you are a heterosexual man, suppose you are going on a blind date and know nothing about your partner except the colour of her hair. How would your expectations vary according to whether she was described as blonde or brunette? Jot down a few traits you might anticipate finding in each woman. Finally, ask yourself which you would prefer to meet.

The stereotype of a blonde (perhaps typified by Marilyn Monroe) is that of a fun-loving, extravert, sexually receptive and desirable woman. On the other hand, as recognised by the popularity of 'blonde' jokes, blondes are regarded as slightly scatty or unintelligent. Brunettes tend to be taken more seriously and for that reason may be preferred as long-term partners or business associates. Some of these ideas may have emerged in your ratings of the traits you anticipated in your date, and whether you preferred the blonde or the brunette might have depended on what kind of relationship or encounter you had hoped for.

Female journalists and others who have changed their hair colour as a social experiment attest to the fact that men (and society in general) treat them differently in accordance with these expectations. They report having 'more proposals and more fun' when in the guise of a blonde, but being shown more respect as a brunette.

There is some truth in the stereotypes relating to women's hair colour as indicated by psychometric personality and ability tests, but since few women are natural blondes beyond a certain age, there is a degree of self-fulfilling prophecy involved – those who want an exciting, sexy lifestyle are more likely to dye their hair blonde. As a result, they are more often invited to parties and attract men wanting short-term flings.

There is, of course, another possibility for women's hair colour, to which certain characteristics are often attached – red hair. Over the years redheads have had something of a bad press, being thought witches in certain times and places. Today they maintain a reputation for being fiery and temperamental and once again the stereotype is vindicated to a degree by personality tests. In other respects, red-heads fall about halfway between blondes and brunettes. We're leaving aside consideration of black hair colour here, because it's so prevalent in many parts of the world as to escape a singular stereotype.

Make-up

Asked what they think of make-up on women, many men claim to prefer the natural look. What they really mean is that the make-up, which is used to disguise blemishes and emphasise feminine facial features, should itself be disguised and not be too obtrusive. Otherwise, there is concern about what the woman might be trying to conceal or about negative self-esteem. Red lipstick, to some people, has clear sexual connotations, dating from the use of carmine by ancient Egyptian prostitutes to advertise oral services. Now it's often worn as a sign of creativity or individuality.

Recent research in the US found that when a woman wears heavy make-up she is inclined to be seen by both men and women as shifty and untrustworthy. It seems we subconsciously think of make-up as a disguise, which suggests that someone is trying to deceive us. On the upside, women wearing make-up were judged as more 'competent' than those without, perhaps because they were seen as taking pride in their appearance.

At present, make-up on men is generally viewed with suspicion despite several attempts by cosmetic companies to normalise it. There are no clear rules about the use of make-up but messages are transmitted whatever choice is made. The absence of make-up may also be a statement – suggesting a down-to-earth, possibly puritanical, woman who prefers no artifice. Obviously, the situation is also important; heavy make-up is more appropriate on an evening out than for an average day at the office or home.

Spectacles

Research shows that people who wear glasses (especially women) are seen as slightly less attractive on average than those who do not. Children in the playground are slightly less popular if they wear glasses and again this applies more so with girls. However, there are also some positive stereotypes associated with wearing glasses. People wearing spectacles are judged as more studious and more intelligent by up to five IQ points. This stereotype is also in place by childhood: eight to ten-year-olds asked to draw 'clever' and 'stupid' persons are more likely to give glasses to the clever one.

People wearing glasses are not only seen as more intelligent; they are also rated as more virtuous. Glasses enhance perceived honesty in both men and women compared with no eyewear. Sunglasses, however, have the opposite effect. They may make us look 'cool' but they create the impression that one is a 'poser' (trying to look like a celebrity), slightly villainous, or with something to hide.

Glasses rank fourth (after sex, race and age) in a hierarchy of salient features in spontaneous verbal descriptions of others. This lessens discriminability and hinders recognition of people wearing glasses. In the situation of having to identify someone it is very hard for people to see past the spectacles, since they stand out in the memory. Not surprisingly, when people want to disguise themselves, spectacles are called upon about as often as wigs and false noses.

Is there any truth to the stereotypes about those who wear glasses? IQ tests show that spectacle-wearers are *actually* more intelligent than non-wearers on average (though not quite to the extent that judgements are affected). It is often supposed that this is because short-sighted people, being poor at sports, develop studious, indoor interests like reading. That may be true, but genes are also involved and the link might have arisen because, before the invention of spectacles, people with poor eyesight needed to be smart to survive. Personality questionnaires confirm that wearers of glasses tend to be more introvert, more conscientious and less open to experience, in line with their 'bookish' rather than outdoor interests.

Facial hair

To shave or not to shave? A man's decision has an important effect upon how others will react to him. Although the impression gained is immediate and felt as instinctive, it actually derives from assessments made about what his motives are and what kind of person he is.

The acceptability and desirability of beards varies from time to time and according to the social context. In ancient Rome only barbarians had beards. In some Muslim societies a beard is a religious requirement. Beards were the norm at certain times in Western history; in the nineteenth century they were a mark of authority and respectability. Today they are associated with particular groups such as naval officers, theatre directors, artists, folk singers and scientists. (Tom Lehrer refers to 'ivy-covered professors in ivy-covered towers'.)

Where there is choice about whether or not to shave, the presence or absence of a beard may be diagnostic of personality, occupation and lifestyle. Some men adopt beards because they believe them to convey a bohemian or intellectual image, signalling that they 'have more to think about than a narcissistic concern with their own looks'. However, more conventional, conservative people tend to view bearded men as unkempt, radical and unreliable. Many reckon that men grow beards to hide something, such as their emotions or a 'weak chin'.

 Any style of facial hair that requires a great deal of upkeep (e.g. Poirot's moustache, or a goatee beard that needs frequent grooming and trimming) transmits a message that is the exact opposite of the abandoned, unshaven hippy. It may, however, come across as precious or obsessional.

Women are divided as to whether they find men with beards attractive but the majority deny that they find them appealing. This is surprising given that gender signals (visual characteristics that differentiate men and women) are usually sexually attractive. Women with big eyes and soft skin are attractive to men, while men with swarthy complexions and strong jaw-lines tend to be attractive to women (especially in the fertile phase of their cycle, when good genes are sought before good husbands). Since facial hair is a testosterone marker, beards ought to be attractive to women. Indeed, it is the association with masculinity that is the reason why British military leaders in the last century sported moustaches and only officers in the British navy had the right to grow beards (lower ranks needed 'permission to strike').

 Despite the survey findings relating to women's attitudes, experimental studies reveal a largely positive view of bearded men. In one American study, women and men were asked to evaluate pictures of college men that varied systematically in amount of facial hair. The same eight young men were photographed at successive phases of depilation – full beard, goatee and moustache, moustache only, and clean-shaven. Generally, the hairier the face the more favourably it was rated. Bearded faces were seen as more mature, good-looking, industrious, creative, self-confident, liberal, non-conforming, courageous, masculine and dominant than shaved faces, by both men and women. The researcher concluded that 'the male beard communicates an heroic image of the independent, sturdy and resourceful pioneer, ready willing and able to do things'.

Other research, however, has turned up negative stereotypes concerning facial hair. Although supporting the masculinity finding, one study found that bearded men were regarded as 'dirtier' and lacking in self-control. Another found clean-shaven men were judged as more trustworthy in certain occupations where this would be a prime consideration (e.g. salesmen). Other findings show that moustaches are usually seen as less attractive than either full beards or clean-shaven faces.

Why men shave

If beards are manly, and frequently seen as attractive, then why do so many men undertake the tedious, time-consuming and hazardous task of daily shaving?

THINK ABOUT IT Anthropologist Desmond Morris said that by showing he has time to spare for toilet rituals a man signals that he is of high status, which naturally appeals to women. This would apply equally to facial hair patterns that require a great deal of attention, as opposed to an unkempt beard. Morris also referred to the ability to transmit more subtle emotions by facial expressions with a clean-shaven face. Others argue that there are advantages to remaining inscrutable, which could be a reason why men have facial hair in the first place (so rivals, partners and poker opponents can't read them so easily).

Shaving creates an impression of trust that women may find particularly attractive in a man. By shaving, a man 'softens' his face so he is seen as less threatening to other males and more of a new man (gentle and empathic) to women. Modern women are not just seeking dominance in male partners; especially when in the non-fertile phase of their cycle, they are at least equally interested in character traits that go with being loyal and supportive partners and fathers. It may also be a matter of hygiene – less food and drink gets stuck around the mouth to breed germs, a particular concern in some occupations, such as surgery and cooking.

The main disadvantage of a beard (apart from hygiene) is that it makes a man look older. Most obviously, the flowing white 'Father Christmas' type of beard ages a man, even though it comes across as friendly and avuncular. God is often portrayed as having this sort of beard, an image emulated by religious gurus around the world. But although age correlates with social power, there usually comes a time in a man's life when he wants to look younger. It is the age factor that probably accounts for the difference in findings between experimental studies (which usually control for age) and surveys (which do not). When only young men are used, more favourable stereotypes of beards emerge, especially as regards sexual attractiveness.

Because there are both advantages and disadvantages to having a beard, some men compromise by trimming their beard fastidiously or cultivating a permanent five-o'clock shadow (sometimes called 'designer stubble'); this permits a display of testosterone without the wearer looking too old (beyond breeding age). In fact, this image (popularised by the likes of Russell Crowe) can make a man look particularly virile because it gives the impression that he does shave, but his beard grows so quickly that he can't keep up.

REMEMBER THIS!!! Stubble is not impressive when respectability is a key consideration, as with politicians seeking election. Richard Nixon notoriously lost to JFK because he declined make-up before a key television debate and his shadowy chin appeared unshaven and untrustworthy.

Changing one's image

Once a beard has been established for whatever reason, it can be quite hard to dispense with. It becomes a 'trademark' – an important part of the man's identity and image. Children often react with distress when their father shaves for the first time after they have become accustomed to a hirsute Daddy. Research confirms that we are more comfortable with people who are familiar-looking, whether we know them very well or have not previously met them.

Of course, some men will grow facial hair or shave off a beard precisely because they want to change their image. This may coincide with some other life change, such as a new partner or career. Alternatively, they may have grown out of the need for the signal (e.g. no longer feeling rebellious or in need of looking sage-like or manly). The ageing biker who continues to sport a walrus beard and leather jacket well into middle age might come across as slightly pathetic. On the other hand, some men perhaps change their style of facial hair rather too frequently, which (like David Beckham's haircuts) suggests insecurity and instability – a quest for an elusive identity that can never quite be satisfied.

Moustaches and sideburns

The moustache is a way of paying 'lip service' to masculinity while at the same time conveying a well-groomed look. But there are many different kinds and styles of moustaches, each with their own stereotype. They may impress as debonair and dashing, hence their popularity with fighter pilots in the Second World War (handlebars), Hollywood leads of the 1950s (Clark Gable), and gay men in the 1970s and 80s (Peter Mandelson ditched his when the signal became dated). The fashion for moustaches in the 1970s appears to have been sparked by certain sportsmen like the American swimmer Mark Spitz and British athletes Daley Thompson and David Bedford. However, a moustache may come across as sinister and untrustworthy – a superficial attempt to seduce or impress (typified by used car salesmen and pantomime villains like Terry-Thomas).

Moustaches make striking trademarks. Hitler, Charlie Chaplin and Groucho Marx are famous examples, even though the latter two mostly just painted them on. It has often been remarked that TV presenter Robert Winston is reminiscent of Groucho, adding a good-humoured touch to his distinctive image. Another iconic moustache is that of Merv Hughes, the macho Australian cricketer whose look continues to be imitated comically by Australian cricket fans today. The moustache was so central to David Bedford's image that he sued British Telecom for using it in their '118 118' campaign.

Sideburns are another way of showing off masculinity while still seeming well-groomed. They were most popular in Victorian and Edwardian (Gilbert and Sullivan) times and came across as affluent and respectable. Today, full sideburns, or 'mutton-chops' as they are known, are very uncommon and suggest old-fashioned eccentricity. Smaller and neater sideburns still make an appearance, however.

Facial hair and the marriage market

One evolutionary psychologist found historical evidence that men are more likely to advertise their masculinity with facial hair when they are having difficulty in obtaining spouses. Records on British facial hair fashions as depicted in the *Illustrated London News* from 1842 to 1971 showed that moustaches (and facial hair generally) were more popular when there was a surplus of single men in society and when illegitimacy rates were high. The conclusion was that men adopt facial hair to enhance their marriage prospects, increasing their attractiveness and apparent social status when partners are in short supply. Other research shows that a fashion for beards correlates with eras in which women wear long skirts (also a sign of austerity?).

Variations in the popularity of facial hair tell us much about a society and its times. Within a given cultural context, however, individual choices tell us much about the message that the wearer intends to convey. Stereotypes concerning the meaning of facial hair patterns may be inaccurate and unjustified in particular instances, but they contain a kernel of truth as generalities, based as they are on experience and observations of personality types.

Summary
Reasons for growing a beard
1. Convenience – dispenses with daily ritual.
2. Sexually attractive to some women.
3. Increase in gravitas – to look older and wiser.
4. Look more masculine and heroic.
5. To conceal emotional expressions.

Reasons for shaving
1. Hygiene – easier to keep face clean.
2. More attractive to some women.
3. Look younger.
4. Look more respectable/trustworthy.
5. More emotionally expressive.

Tattoos and piercings

While the stereotypes of facial hair are mixed and situation-dependent, those of tattoos and piercings can be fairly negative (except perhaps among people who actually sport them). These 'adornments' may be perceived as threatening, desperate, nihilistic, and indicative of anti-social traits like criminality, drug addiction and sexual perversion (much like the reactions to scars). At best, people with tattoos and piercings are seen by the general population as tough and independent; at worst they are seen as dangerous delinquents or self-absorbed fantasists.

There was a time when tattoos were almost exclusive to sailors trying to assert their manhood, or too drunk to protest when their mates pushed them to 'join the club'. In some areas, they have become badges of gang membership and flags of the capacity to be dangerous – 'not to be messed with'. Sometimes they appear as a kind of graffiti carried on the body, which include messages ranging from the name of a partner or child to the expression of far-right political views.

Today there is a trend towards more artistic patterns in tattoos and piercings and a growing fashionability among young people. Current estimates suggest that one-fifth of Britons, and the same proportion of Americans, has a tattoo. The numbers increase to one in three Britons between the ages of sixteen and 44. This means that the image of such adornments is improving among certain circles but their generally negative image has not been totally reversed among the wider population.

 Those who choose to be tattooed or pierced should be aware that messages are often conveyed beyond those intended, and their permanence results in many regretting their decision to have them early in life. For example, the name of the boy/girlfriend may have changed or they have children and need to find a job that requires a clean-cut image.

Impressing in a job interview

A situation in which first impressions are particularly important is that of the job interview. Job selection interviews typically last for about half an hour but research shows that most of the decisions are made within the first four minutes, far too soon for personality and intelligence to be properly assessed. This is so even when the employer has not seen the application form and has no prior knowledge of the candidate. In fact, what the interviewer thinks of the candidate's appearance (before they have said anything at all) predicts the final decision 80% of the time. Obviously, this snap judgement must be made on the basis of superficial appearance and mannerisms.

Among the characteristics that emerge as favourable are self-assurance, eye contact, enthusiasm, cologne, a firm handshake and spectacles (probably for their effect on apparent IQ and conscientiousness). Tattoos, piercings and scars are especially detrimental. Among other pet hates of interviewers (though not all) are smoking, unkempt hair and beards, dirty fingernails, scuffed shoes and extreme haircuts/colouring. Humour may be beneficial but not if it comes across as smart-arse, competitive or hostile.

 Mirroring the body language of the interviewers may be a way of increasing rapport and making them feel more receptive towards you. However, care must be taken that it is subtle and does not come across as mocking. Also, if you are getting cold and negative signals from the panel the last thing you want to do is reciprocate them.

In most matters it is a question of achieving a proper balance between extremes. A firm handshake means neither flabby nor knuckle-crunching. Warm signals, like smiles and nods of agreement, are generally good, up to the point where they might seem weak or ingratiating. It is best not to seem overly serious, but nor should one adopt a permanent silly grin. Overly casual postures such as leaning back in the chair and crossing the legs so that one ankle rests on a knee will appear sloppy or impertinent. Self-assurance is good up to the point where the boss is threatened by overconfidence and pushiness. After all, your employer wants to remain boss after he/she has taken you on.

Dress should be neat, fashionable and appropriate, showing that an effort has been made to be respectful but without seeming overly 'fussy'. Men should dress so that their clothes do not upstage their personality and distract from what they have to say. Lighter clothes often give a younger, more relaxed appearance. Natural fibres, like cotton and wool, give a better impression than most man-made fibres and of course they should be clean and properly pressed. Women should dress so as to be neither too severe nor too flighty, and should generally favour more conservative rather than revealing clothing. A low-cut dress is unlikely to go down well in an interview for a business executive role.

The important thing about dress is that it be appropriate to the occasion and to the job. A bow tie, for example, would seem slightly peculiar if one was applying to be an office cleaner. Bank clerks are expected to be conservative and reliable, whereas designers would be expected to show some flair for style and colour. In other jobs, such as scientific research, there may be no clear expectation about how a candidate would dress since it is largely irrelevant.

1. It may be worth hanging around outside the desired workplace to scout out how current employees are presenting themselves before appearing for your interview; this might help you blend with the culture and look as though you would 'fit in'.

2. Stylish dress is important but designer labels do not necessarily impress in a creative context in which individuality is valued. You should be seen to have made an effort to impress without appearing to be a 'fashion victim'.

3. Avoid jangling, ostentatious jewellery because it is distracting and may come across as venal. Bling on a man definitely creates a bad impression in most contexts.

4. Wearing a watch is fine but don't keep looking at it as though you are anxious for the interview to be over.

5. Make-up can often be a matter of taste, and open to different interpretations, so you might want to keep it subtle, except in creative companies or where your research (Tip 1) suggests it will be appropriate.

6. Talk with a comfortable tempo – too fast sounds nervous and you might lose the audience, too slow can come across as dull-witted.

7. Avoid negative body language such as avoidance of eye contact, touching the face, looking at the ground,

and slumping in the chair. As a rule of thumb, it is best to maintain eye contact for about one third of the time during an interview. Much less seems awkward and furtive; much more might be threatening.

8. Keep an appropriate distance from the interviewing panel; if you are close enough for them to smell last night's garlic on your breath you are crowding them.

9. Try to make the panel like you, using genuine smiles.

10. Be attentive and connect with what they are saying (see Chapter 4).

How to hitch a ride

Being a successful hitch-hiker is a bit like applying for a short-term job (that of companion to a lonely driver). Furthermore, it is a situation where first impressions are critical, since a driver has only a split second to decide whether or not to stop. Clearly, any danger signals like tattoos, scars and piercings will deter drivers, whereas respectable dress might swing it positively. They may even think it is a fellow driver who has broken down and needs a ride to a service station. As noted above, be careful of using the thumb-thrusting gesture to request a lift; in certain countries, such as Greece, it may be seen as an obscene gesture.

One study of hitch-hiker success concluded that eye contact was the key factor in getting a driver to stop. This could be because it signals trustworthiness and arouses empathy. However, cause and effect goes both ways and drivers who have no intention of stopping usually avoid eye contact (rather as they do with 'squeegee' merchants). Female hitch-hikers may come across as less threatening and so have greater success in catching a ride, though they should take extra care in choosing lifts if hiking alone.

---

3. Let's face it

Primates spend more time than other animals in face-to-face contact with each other – and humans especially so. This is probably the reason why the muscles of our face are so highly developed as a system for signalling feelings and attitudes. Smiling, for example, is one of the clearest ways of showing friendly intent, while frowning is an obvious way of communicating annoyance. However, it should be realised that while facial movements 'betray' emotions unintentionally, others are used just for emphasis and therefore function more like hand gestures.

Californian psychologist Dr Paul Ekman reckons it is possible to create 7,000 different patterns of the facial muscles, each having its own shade of meaning. He identifies a number of common groupings called 'action units' (e.g. the 'nose-wrinkler', the 'cheek raiser', the 'dimpler' and the 'lip corner puller'). Each of these involves several muscles but they tend to work in concert and so help to simplify analysis of how emotional expression is generated.

Seven key emotions and related facial signals

Happiness – cheeks are raised and lip corners pulled causing folds and dimples to form from the nostrils out beyond the lips and from the eyes out to the cheeks.

Sadness – raised eyebrows with forehead wrinkles that slope down from the centre.

Anger – lowered eyebrows, a hard stare, lips pressed tightly together or slightly open to give a square-shaped mouth.

Fear – eyes widen, with whites more apparent. Corners of lips move back so mouth opens slightly.

Surprise – raised eyebrows and upper eyelids, horizontal wrinkles on forehead, mouth usually open. (Similar to fear but more short-lived.)

Disgust – wrinkled nose and raised upper lip, mouth curled with lip corners pulled back and down.

Contempt – corner of one lip tightens and rises slightly; like a sneer but without the wrinkled nose of disgust.

Other important facial signals

Smiling – teeth together, lips parted slightly, relaxed expression.

Laughing – eyes crinkle as with smile, but teeth are parted and partially covered by lips.

Submission – broad grin, gums showing, apprehension around eyes.

Greeting – smile and eyebrow 'flash' (raised briefly).

Interest – eyes wide open, but may squint to focus on distant objects.

Blinking – may indicate tension or lying, decreases during concentration.

Pupil dilation – showing attraction or interest (or just a response to dim light).

CASE STUDY

Wistful Woody
The comedian Woody Allen is often seen to raise the inner ends of his eyebrows as a form of emphasis in conversation. This gives him a characteristic look of melancholy. Since this is difficult to manufacture consciously, it supports Allen's description of himself as inclined towards misanthropy and depression (a negative, cynical view of life that is frequently manifested in his comedy). Something similar is depicted in the sad equivalent of the 'smiley face' icon on a computer, which has eyebrows that slope down on each side from the centre of the brow.

Recent research has found that what makes a face look sinister is a large pointed chin and prominent eyebrows that slope downwards towards the centre, almost converging. This is seen in the classic cartoon character 'baddies' such as Captain Hook, Dick Dastardly and Cruella De Vil. It has also been found that people are more sensitive to negative faces, picking sad and angry expressions out of a crowd more quickly than positive ones. This is perhaps because we use them as indicators of threat. Quite what we can do to avoid looking evil is difficult to say, other than to trim our eyebrows so that any downward shape is less apparent and to try to maintain a happy face.

Reading faces is tricky

Although faces are highly expressive they can also be deceptive and difficult to read. This is because people are often themselves in a conflict about how they should react and their mixed feelings result in ambiguous signals. It is common, for example, for a threat signal to combine both hostility and fear, as though the individual is unsure as to whether fight or flight is the better option. When the urge to attack predominates the frown is deeper, the mouth tightly compressed, the head thrust forward and the skin whiter. When a greater amount of fear is present in the mix, the eyes are open and staring and the mouth shows a snarl that reveals more teeth.

Faces may be hard to read because humans are complex social animals that have learned to suppress the display of emotions for various reasons. It is often inappropriate to show negative emotions like hatred and contempt in public, so people go about wearing socially acceptable faces rather like masks.

 Since humans are able to control their mouth signals more easily than their eyes and forehead, the top half of the face usually provides a more valid reading of emotion. A false smile, for example, can be detected because it is restricted to the mouth region and does not extend to the eyes.

Women are generally more intuitive about reading the faces of others but they are also easier to read (by both men and women). This is because women tend to be more emotionally expressive. If men and women are asked to imagine situations that might be expected to induce happiness, sadness, anger, fear, etc. (e.g. 'you inherit a million dollars'; 'your mother dies'; 'someone bashes into your car by driving recklessly'), then women show more muscle activity in their face. Interestingly, they also report a more vivid experience of the emotion, so it is likely that women express more emotion because they feel more emotion.

Smiling women

Take an ordinary newspaper and count the number of women pictured smiling or not, then do the same for men. Calculating percentages for each sex should reveal that women characteristically smile more often than men. Do women smile more because they have learned to be 'pleasant' and appeasing, or are they warmer and more agreeable on average? Does the newspaper reflect an accurate spread of society, or does it choose more images of serious-looking men and happy-looking women? Or do the images reflect a wider social bias, by which more men still hold 'serious' roles of power and more women hold roles in which they need to be more agreeable?

Miles of smiles

A smile generally comes across as warm and friendly but it can project a lot of other feelings besides. If used inappropriately it can appear silly, as when a woman is photographed smiling even though her husband has just been convicted of mass murder. It can also express submissiveness by showing that our teeth are not open and geared for biting. It can betray insincerity if it fails to include the eyes (as mentioned above) or because it is switched on and off too quickly.

Franz Lehar wrote an operetta called *The Land of Smiles* referring to China, where the multiplicity of different smiles and their various meanings are legend. But there are many different types of smile in Western countries also. Some of those identified by observers are as follows:

1. The upper smile – lips are parted to show only the upper teeth. A warm social smile used in greeting and friendly conversation. Associated with eye contact and used to cement mother/child and other bonding.

2. The shy smile – similar, but lower lip is tucked in behind the teeth and the head is tilted down slightly. Used by

adults when embarrassed but still in good humour and infants encountering a strange adult.

3. The false smile – like upper smile but lacks tiny pouches under the eyes and crinkling at the corners. Appears when bored at a social function or when posing awkwardly in photos. Can easily turn into a contemptuous sneer if the lip is pulled up actively.

4. The broad smile – lower teeth are bared in addition to the upper ones. Occurs when someone is seen to trip, when being tickled, or laughing at a joke. Because it has aggressive overtones it tends to be suppressed into an upper smile when eye contact is made with other people.

5. The oblong smile – mouth corners are squared, showing gritted teeth. Reflects a mixture of aggression and fear, or assertiveness and appeasement, e.g., when dealing with a drunk.

6. The play smile – mouth wide open with corners drawn up, but teeth remain hidden. Seen in children enjoying games and adults awaiting a comedian's next joke.

7. The simple smile – mouth corners move out and up, lips are slightly stretched but remain relaxed and do not part. Occurs when smiling to oneself in private or recalling an amusing, happy event.

8. The wry smile – like the simple smile but mouth corners are turned down in a lopsided, scowl-like formation. Seen when we are disconcerted or disapproving but not seriously annoyed.

9. The compressed smile – lips are pressed together tightly and the corners of the mouth move outward and up. Used as mild social warning, as when someone tells us a joke that we think is in bad taste.

Smiling versus laughing

Many people think of laughing as a more extreme form of smiling but their instinctive origins are quite separate. The smile derives from a submissive, appeasement gesture in non-human primates. The mouth is stretched back so as to reveal the teeth closed in a non-threatening position, essentially saying, 'See, I'm totally harmless and won't bite you'. The laugh is nearer to an aggressive signal, like that of a monkey that shows its teeth open and ready to bite, while making a loud glottal 'ah-ah-ah' sound to threaten a rival. This is especially true of the kind of laugh that children use when ridiculing one another in the playground and when adults make hostile jokes against ethnic out-groups. Naturally enough, the appeasing smile has been adopted by humans to signal friendly intent.

Another form of laughter stems from tension relief and is nearer to crying; it begins as a modification of the laugh that occurs when an infant recognises its mother and danger is suddenly dissipated. An instance was noted when a pilot had crashed his small plane through a barn on a farmstead and was found sitting in the cockpit laughing his head off; he was not laughing because it was funny so much as with the relief at coming out of it unscathed.

Laugh and be merry

If you contrive to pull your face artificially into the shape of a smile you are almost certain to start feeling happier. It is extremely hard to be angry or miserable with a smile on your face. Try watching a very funny cartoon with a pen held between your lips for a while. Now try holding the pen between your teeth. The cartoon is likely to seem funnier when your mouth is held open by the pen in the latter condition. Being tight-lipped is bound to inhibit our experience of humour.

People are two-faced

If you take a photo of a person and draw a dividing line down the centre of the face the two sides will often look different. Generally, the left side is more emotionally expressive. An emotion portrayed by an actor is more easily identified in the left half of the face than the right. The likely reason is that the right half of the brain 'feels' emotions more strongly than the relatively cold, logical left side and since the right side of the brain controls the muscles on the left side of the face the feelings are exhibited more on that side. The right side of the brain is also the reservoir of facial configurations and hence creates them more effectively in the face. You can try this with a photo of yourself; you might expect to see a stronger expression on the left side of your face, regardless of what that expression is (whether happy, sad or angry).

There is some evidence that the left–right differences in facial expression are more striking when the emotion is simulated than when it is real. Heartfelt emotion seems to be more evenly distributed across the face than when it has been manufactured deliberately. Paul Ekman maintains that separate neural pathways are involved in conscious expression compared with that which is spontaneous and hence more sincere. He believes that manufactured expressions derive from the outer layer of the brain (the cerebral cortex) whereas true emotion is generated from more central (limbic) regions of the brain. It follows that large differences in the expressiveness of the two sides of the face tend to betray insincerity.

THINK ABOUT IT

Wisconsin psychologist Karl Smith found that people can be classified according to which side of their face is dominant. The majority (around 85%) are right-faced, with only a minority of around 15% being left-faced (similar to left-handedness). In Smith's research, dominance was measured by recording facial muscle responses but it can also be seen just by looking at the face. The dominant side is described as larger and more muscular, more flexible during speech and with a deeper dimple when smiling. The face appears more open on the dominant side, with a higher brow, and a tendency to tilt towards the listener when speaking. The mouth tends to open wider on the dominant side when speaking.

Smith says that whereas most people are right-faced, musicians (including composers, singers and orchestral musicians) are more often left-faced. Presumably this signifies a more developed right hemisphere of the brain, which mediates many aspects of musical processing. By contrast, mathematicians, scientists, athletes, politicians, newscasters and actors are especially likely to be right-faced according to Smith, because they depend more on thinking than feeling, and are good with speech, which is controlled by the left side of the brain.

Is there a side to you?
Take a look at yourself in the mirror. Which side of your face is longer from the chin to the eyebrow? Which side is more muscular and smooth? Which side of your mouth opens more when you talk and tilts towards the person listening? If these are mostly consistent then that side of your face is dominant. Don't forget that because you are looking in a mirror your face is reversed compared to a photograph and the way

others see you. If you are left-faced you might well be musically talented; if right-faced your occupation is likely to depend more on speaking and numerical skills.

At first blush

Many people are embarrassed because their face is inclined to go red when they are in social difficulty. They should be reassured that this is not unattractive, particularly in women where it is likely to be interpreted as a modesty signal. If there has been an actual social transgression then the blushing may serve as a form of apology that has an appeasing effect (e.g. 'I didn't mean to spill wine on your lovely white carpet – it was an accident that I sincerely regret').

Flushing of the face is somewhat different from blushing. It tends to occur when one is angry and has come close to an actual attack. What happens is that blood is redirected towards the muscles that would be deployed in a fight, causing the face to be drained so it looks white. If the attack is aborted there is a rebound effect, with the blood rushing back to the face. This may still function as a threat signal to an enemy who may realise that they almost pushed it too far. In the case of blushing, this rebound comes following a momentary urge to flee from social attention (which would also involve muscular action). Hence flushing suggests aggression while blushing suggests fear and submissiveness. It may be difficult to separate them except by background circumstances.

Here's looking at you

The eyes are the most powerful social signallers that we have and hence are sometimes called 'the windows of the soul'. This is why we pay so much attention to another person's eyes when we look at them and interact with them. One of the key elements of what is called 'social skills training' is getting just the right amount of eye contact. Too little and we come across as shy and awkward; too much and we seem rude.

The use of gaze is especially important in conversation. People normally look into each other's eyes about one third of the time. Much less suggests boredom, inattention or guilt; much more may be threatening. But this is a rough and ready average and there are meaningful variations.

1. We make more eye contact when listening than when talking.

2. A glance at the other may be used to 'pass the ball' of conversation, effectively saying: 'I've finished, what do you think about that?'

3. Friendly people look into the eyes of the other more than those that are unfriendly.

4. Lovers gaze into each other's eyes to express intimacy and dilate their pupils when interested and aroused.

5. There are cultural differences (e.g. Italians look longer than the English, hence think of them as cold, while the English regard the Italians as over-familiar).

6. Women use gaze more than men, especially when they are in love or captivated by them in some way. We noted in Chapter 1 that the tendency for women to make eye contact with a man and then divert their gaze away is a 'modesty' ritual with flirtatious connotations. It is not generally seen as appropriate between straight men.

Visual chicken

Try staring mutually into the eyes of a friend with the challenge of who can maintain the gaze longest before opting out. This 'battle of the eyes' is a game that is often played in school playgrounds. It is a disquieting experience that may at some point break down into mutual laughter, but it is interesting to analyse who wins and why. Submissive people and those who feel outranked are more likely to back down. In real life the loser probably spends more time looking at his/her feet than gazing directly at other people.

Eye contact can be used either as a means of seeking intimacy or as an attempt to intimidate. By corollary, avoidance of eye contact may be a means of avoiding excessive intimacy or an act of social submission. In many cultures, commoners are not permitted to make eye contact with royalty (though 'a cat can look at a queen'). It may be dangerous to make eye contact with gang members in an inner city street and certain Hollywood stars are reputed to issue instructions that film crew and extras are not to catch their eye on set because they find it offputting.

REMEMBER THIS!!!

Women in 'a man's world'

Women who want to establish authority in relationships with men, whether at work or socially, may need to deliberately adopt a more male style in the use of gaze. For example, they might make eye contact for shorter periods of time in conversation and avoid flirtatious signals. Similarly, men who want to avoid coming across as cold and superior in their dealings with women may soften themselves by adopting more warm and supportive patterns of eye contact in the workplace and elsewhere.

---

4. Do you like me?

One of the most important things to know about another person is whether or not they like us. This will determine the future of our relationship with them, regardless of whether they are potential business contacts, friends or lovers. They may be blunt enough to just say outright that they find us interesting and attractive or boring and repugnant, but that is uncommon. More likely they will conceal their feelings to some degree, leaving us to read their body language in order to assess what they think of us.

There are some social rituals such as handshakes, embraces, greetings and gifts that might give us a clue as to how we are regarded. If they are deliberately withheld then it might be deemed insulting and the message will be obvious, but usually we have to evaluate the manner in which they are conducted. Other useful signals of warmth and coldness can be more subtle but equally revealing.

Some warm signals
1. Eye contact – especially if slightly extended, indicates that the other person is interested.

2. Pupil dilation – this suggests particular interest, perhaps even romantic attraction.

3. Attentiveness – listening carefully to what you have to say is a positive sign (as opposed to looking over your

shoulder to see if there is someone more interesting about).

4. Smiling and laughing – generally signify warmth, even though there are certain types of laugh that border on the hostile.

5. Proximity – generally speaking, people who like us get close and do not back off if we approach them.

6. Body orientation – people who like us orient their body towards us. Their feet point towards us as though they are inclined to move in our direction. When seated they cross their legs so their body is open towards us, not forming a barrier against us.

7. Preening – various self-grooming behaviours like adjusting clothes and hair, standing tall and pulling in the stomach are flirtatious and suggest sexual attraction.

8. Grooming another – if attention is made towards improving the presentation of the other person (e.g. adjusting their clothing or picking off lint) this is even more suggestive of attraction.

9. Excited movement – if a person cannot stay still in your presence, shows faster breathing, flushed face and minor accident-proneness they are probably anxious to make a good impression.

10. Ownership signals – finding a pretext to put a hand on your shoulder or an arm around you, or surrounding you in such a way as to exclude others from conversation, indicates strong interest.

11. Mirroring – when another person imitates our gestures shortly after we make them, they are showing us that they are 'in tune'. Even walking in step is a positive sign.

12. Exposing the vulnerable parts – if someone exposes their wrists, leans their head back to make their neck open to you, or opens their arms so that the front of their body is accessible, this is a sign of trust.

13. There are various other gestures that carry specific connotations of sexual invitation (e.g. lip smacking, crotch displays, stroking the thighs, loosening the shoes, arranging one's hands so that they point towards the genitals, and fondling phallic objects like a salt cellar).

Some cold signals

Virtually all the warm signals listed above can be put into reverse so as to be signs of rejection.

1. Avoidance – If, instead of getting close to you, the other person moves backwards as though you are talking too loud or have bad breath, then they are clearly not looking to further a friendship.

2. Frowning is the opposite of a smile. Various forms of sickly smile suggest that one is trying to appear warm but having great difficulty in doing so.

3. Screwing up the eyes – unless the light is excessively bright this is equivalent to blotting out the sight of another person, indicating you would rather they were not there.

4. Turning away – an obvious way of being cold is to transfer attention to someone else in a social situation. Looking over a person's shoulder in conversation has the same effect.

5. Barrier signals – if another person folds their arms across their chest so as to shut you out and deny you access to the front of their body, then they are indicating resistance either to you personally or to your ideas. Holding a lit cigarette or a glass of drink out in front of one's body may also be a way of fending people off.

6. Closing out – if when sitting beside another person the legs are crossed so that the one on the top creates a barrier, this suggests a kind of resistance.

7. Wiping a finger across the nose is a specific gesture that suggests the other is in some way unclean or undesirable.

8. Biting the lip – also a negative sign, indicating that one would like to bite the other person or is suppressing an abusive verbal outburst.

9. Picking imaginary lint off one's own clothes conveys the message that one is bored with the other (wants to be rid of pests).

10. A sneer, a pout, a fake yawn or a cold stare are other obvious negative facial gestures.

11. Various distraction activities such as fidgeting, picking the teeth, cleaning the finger nails, playing with split ends, chewing gum, chain smoking and cracking the fingers also signal rejection.

Clearly, there is an opposite pole to most of the warm signals listed previously that can give the clue that you are not well received. Interestingly, some gestures that we would normally think of as intimate can be used in such a way as to signal the opposite. For example, the double-sided air kiss is a way of expressing distance because it avoids lip contact and is reduced to a ritual 'going through the motions'. Even a one-sided peck on the cheek is usually warmer because there is an opportunity for more prolonged contact and is more like the sort of kiss a parent would give to a loved child.

Blair and Brown

It is widely acknowledged that there was personal antipathy between the two Labour leaders Gordon Brown and Tony Blair throughout Blair's premiership. Oxford psychologist Peter Collett confirmed this in a body language analysis of Gordon Brown as he listened to Blair's speech to the Labour Party Conference in 2003. Although making a show of support for Blair by nodding avidly, Brown's smile was more of a sickly grimace. From the moment Blair appeared at the podium, Brown began emitting negative signals, looking down at the ground and pressing his tongue against his cheek. In the course of an hour, he adjusted his clothes 25 times, bit his lip 12 times, touched his face 35 times, fiddled with his cuffs 29 times, crossed his arms 36 times and looked away 155 times. Of the 322 discomfort signs shown by Brown, most occurred more markedly when the audience was clapping and cheering Blair. He was usually the last to begin clapping his rival and the first to finish.

Mirroring

Reflecting the body language of another person is one of the most interesting indicators of warmth because it can be deliberately manipulated to make another person feel comfortable. Also called 'synchrony' or 'postural echo', mirroring refers to the fact that when two people are in harmony they tend to imitate each other's postures and gestures. For the most part it is unconscious and it conveys the silent message, 'See, I'm just like you, so you can relax in my company'. Research in singles bars shows that mirroring is a particularly good predictor of who will go off together, whereas a breakdown in synchrony usually heralds the end of an encounter.

 Analysis of who is mirroring whom indicates which of the pair is dominant. Generally, the person who initiates changes in posture that are copied by the other person is the one who is dominant in the relationship. However, there may be circumstances in which a high-status individual deliberately mirrors a subordinate in order to put them at their ease (in a job interview for example).

If mirroring is used as a deliberate ploy then it needs to be done with caution. If it becomes obvious to the other (e.g. in a singles bar situation) it would appear ludicrous or deviant and might backfire seriously. If the body language of a boss is meant to convey dominance (e.g. sprawling back in his chair and putting his feet up on the desk to make it clear that he owns the place) then reciprocation on the part of the employee would come across as challenging and impertinent, perhaps leading to dismissal.

Although mirroring implies a shared attitude, that attitude is not necessarily a positive one. 'Cold mirroring' also occurs, as when a couple turn their back on one another so as to create mutual barriers. Obviously, if you want to appease another person or get them on side, you do not echo their hostile signals.

 Sales staff are sometimes taught that mirroring a prospective customer is an effective way of ingratiating themselves. Again, it needs to be very discreet and it applies only to warm signals. Mirroring dominance gestures is likely to turn a friendly encounter into a power struggle. Salespeople sometimes watch a couple to see which of the two initiates gestures that are copied by the other. This provides a clue as to which is dominant, so that the sales pitch can be focused towards that member of the pair.

Courtship signals

When a couple is courting all of the warm signals are magnified.

1. They gaze into each other's eyes with dilated pupils.

2. They listen attentively and divulge intimate, personal details.

3. They smile and laugh a lot.

4. They mirror each other's movements.

5. They tighten their body muscles to pull themselves upright and appear more youthful and vigorous.

6. Their head is tilted back to give an impression of extra height and balletic lightness.

7. They orient themselves full-on to their partner with their feet pointed towards them and surround them in such a way as to exclude intruders.

8. They expose vulnerable parts of their body (such as wrist and neck).

9. Because one is pursuing the other (or just to burn off adrenaline) their excitement may cause them to rotate in a slow, circling 'dance', while maintaining their face-to-face orientation.

10. They preen and groom: e.g. they make little adjustments to their clothing, like straightening their tie or playing with the buttons of their blouse, and they play with their hair.

Intimate gestures

1. In later stages of a relationship a couple will groom each other as much as themselves. For example, a woman may adjust her man's tie or dust his lapel, or a man may brush the hair away from his woman's eyes ('mothering' gestures usually reserved for someone special).

2. The intimate couple will talk in soft, low tones and whisper sweet nothings.

3. They use baby talk that revives memories of parental care and devotion.

4. They advertise their bond by holding hands and putting their arms around each other.

5. They gaze into each other's eyes and seem oblivious to everyone and everything around them.

6. They find excuses to touch each other, or just touch each other for no apparent reason.

7. They kiss deeply, mouth-to-mouth (see Chapter 8).

Fear of rejection

When trying to interpret someone's body language and assess whether they are attracted to us there is a danger of over-simplifying. While it is generally true that when people approach us, smile, make eye contact, touch us, etc. it means that they like us, there are some exceptions. The interaction between a pair of strangers who are mutually attracted usually proceeds with caution, each party looking for signs of reciprocation and reassurance before moving on to the next step.

 We all have an ego and fear rejection to a greater or lesser extent and this may sometimes cause us to do the opposite of what would be expected. One or the other may 'play hard to get' or use some such paradoxical strategy ('people think I'm funny when I insult them'). Behaviour like this can make it difficult to read the body language of attraction. Fortunately, most people are too excited when they meet someone attractive to cloud the issue with psychological games.

Gender differences

The classic courtship behaviours show some differences between men and women. Men are more likely to pull their stomach in and stretch themselves to full height, trying to look tall. They confront their 'quarry' in a more aggressive way, so as to make escape or intrusion from rivals more difficult. They fix them with a steady gaze and adopt a cowboy pose – spreading their legs wide apart and drawing attention to their genital area by thrusting their thumbs inside their belt so their fingers point towards their crotch.

Women are often more subtle, making contact briefly with their eyes, then averting them. They make the vulnerable parts of their body more open to the person who appeals to them, e.g. their wrists, neck and genital area. The moisten their lips with their tongue and leave their mouth slightly open (in a manner symbolising the genitals). They preen – for example, tossing their hair back off their face in a haughty, animal kind of way.

Am I boring you?

It is useful to know when we might be boring someone we have met at a party or social event. The usual signs are approximation to sleep – such things as closing or glazing of the eyes, stretching, yawning, body slumping or resting the head suggest that alertness is slipping. Of course the other person may simply be short of sleep after a late night, and yawning is not only a sign of boredom. It is socially contagious and may just mean that the person is relaxed in your company. Nevertheless, we need to be aware of the possibility that we are boring the other person.

 Lint picking (removing tiny bits of fluff, which might be imaginary, from one's clothing) may signify boredom. However, it can also signal disagreement or disapproval in a situation where the lint-picker feels unable to express a negative opinion or to make an escape – for example, when the boss is giving his political views at an office party. Squirming in the chair may be a similar sign of general unease when there is a suppressed desire to escape from an unpleasant entrapment.

Note that, as mentioned above, when someone else picks lint off our clothing it usually has the opposite meaning. In this case it is a kind of grooming, such as a mother would perform on her child, and it may signify sexual attraction.

What makes us boring?

Research at the University of North Carolina has identified some of the behaviours that make people boring. These are assembled in the following league table:

1. Complaining – droning on about personal problems, especially minor illnesses like varicose veins.

2. Banality – talking about superficial things; telling the same bad joke over and over.

3. Emotional flatness – speaking monotonously, lacking facial expression and avoiding eye contact.

4. Tediousness – dragging out conversations; taking too long to come to the point.

5. Passivity – excessive conformity and reluctance to express novel opinions.

6. Self-preoccupation – talking incessantly about oneself.

7. Seriousness – taking everything seriously and never lightening the conversion with a smile or a joke.

8. Ingratiation – sucking up and trying to be excessively friendly.

9. Distraction – being easily distracted by what is going on around.

10. Too much use of jargon and slang.

None of these is particularly surprising and they may be difficult to override if we are naturally lacking in charisma. However, it is useful to monitor ourselves from time to time to see whether our traits might be driving others away.

Are they sexually attracted to me?

If we have just met somebody for the first time (at a party for example) and they are instantly attracted to us, what we might observe are signs of agitation, nervousness and flustering:

1. Their heart is beating faster.

2. They become flushed in the face and neck.

3. Their breathing is faster and heavier.

4. The pupils of their eyes widen.

5. They may shuffle their feet.

6. They twiddle their fingers nervously.

7. They become confused and tongue-tied; conversation is awkward and stilted.

8. They may be accident-prone – e.g. spilling their drink or missing their mouth with the peanuts.

9. The various courtship gestures described above (smiling, preening and self-grooming, etc.) are evident.

THINK ABOUT IT Note that many of these nervous signs overlap with what is observed when another person is frightened of you. In a sense they are – frightened that they will make a fool of themselves and not make a good impression.

When a person is sexually attracted to us they will often make excuses to touch us. For example, they place a hand on our arm with the excuse that they are guiding us, towards the bar or perhaps to introduce us to someone else. The tenderness and warmth by which this is done can tell us a great deal. An obvious pretext for body contact is an invitation to dance. If they are attracted they will stay close to the other person afterwards rather than moving off with some excuse the moment the music stops. When people complain that their feet are killing them, say they have to get back to their friends, or that they need to go to the toilet, the chances are they are not that into us. However, the possibility should also be considered that they are just terribly shy and insecure.

Some forms of touching have a possessive aspect to them. When a hand is placed on a partner's knee a statement is being made to others present as well as the partner themselves: 'This one is mine – keep off.'

Tips on how to make someone like you

1. Tell yourself that you really like the other person. This will come through in the warmth of your smile, handshake, etc. (In the theatre it is called 'method acting'.)

2. Make friendly (non-threatening) eye contact and look them over appreciatively.

3. Remember their name and make a point of using it from time to time (without overdoing it).

4. Take an interest in everything about them – what they have to say and what they like to do. Smile and make eye contact at the moment when they have just said something witty or amusing.

5. Agree with most of their opinions without seeming sycophantic and be careful about how you express disagreements.

6. Lean in towards the other person and point your feet in their direction.

7. Echo their postures and gestures, again without being so obvious that it comes across as 'mocking'.

8. Be happy, relaxed and 'yourself' in their company. The latter is particularly important because if you cannot be yourself it is usually best not to pursue a friendship. You are bound to be 'found out' sometime.

5. Lie to me

In the TV series of this name, Dr Cal Lightman (Tim Roth) is a trained psychologist with an uncanny talent for spotting deception, which he deploys on various government assignments and in support of the law enforcement agencies. Although coming across as almost psychic, he in fact applies various well-established principles of body language and his skill is just a finely honed version of one we all possess to a greater or less degree.

Spotting the liar

There is a fun parlour game that can be played with any number of people and which has been adopted as a TV game show. One individual tells three short and unlikely stories concerning experiences they have had in the past. One of the three stories is a total fabrication. The others have to guess which of the stories is the deception. They may back up their guesses with the observations they used to make their selection. In another version of this game, the fictional event is provided to the individual as a written account that they read before presenting the three stories.

Try playing this game with your family and friends. How reliably are you able to tell which story is false? What cues were you using to detect the lie? Do you think it matters whether the person telling the stories is a good actor?

How can we tell if someone is lying?

This is a question that concerns many people: the jealous spouse looking for evidence of cheating in their partner, the detective investigating a crime by interviewing witnesses, the jury assessing the guilt of the accused, and the political leader trying to anticipate the intentions of his/her enemies. In everyday situations, such as buying a used car or interviewing a candidate for a job, it is also useful to assess people's sincerity.

A variety of non-verbal cues (or 'tells') may be used to assess truthfulness. These have been studied in experiments conducted by psychologists in which people are asked to try to get away with deception rather in the manner of the parlour game described above. They may be asked to role-play a person smuggling drugs past a 'customs inspector', or a doctor lying to a 'patient' about the severity of their symptoms. Of course, in the real world the stakes are usually much higher, so some sort of motivation might have to be introduced such as framing it as a test of skill or by offering a monetary reward for successful deception. Other studies are based on famous instances of people who in retrospect are known to have been lying, with an examination of the non-verbal behaviour that might have given them away.

The 'leakage' of untruth

The secret of detecting lying is to look for signs of 'leakage'. This refers to information that is transmitted despite the best efforts of the sender to suppress or camouflage the signals. For example, a false smile is distinguishable because it appears only around the mouth and does not affect the muscles around the eyes. There is an absence of crinkling around and under the eyes, which could result from Botox or cosmetic surgery, but is much more often a mark of insincerity. A false smile is also inclined to be crooked (non-symmetrical from left to right), making it appear warped and sickly. It is also turned on and off too quickly, like a light switch.

When people try to conceal their emotions they often succeed quite well in controlling their face but give themselves away with body movements. Deception is often betrayed by unnecessary movements of the hand towards the face. These hand-to-face movements may be understood as partial attempts to cover the mouth because it is felt to be a giveaway area or even to prevent it from lying in the first place. After all, we have been taught from an early age that lying is wrong. Touching the nose, stroking the chin or pulling at the earlobe may be deflected attempts to cover the lie by some part of the brain that feels guilt or conflict regarding the deception. It is as though the hand has come up spontaneously to cover the face (especially the mouth) and then has to find some other excuse for being there.

The Pinocchio effect
Another reason why people who are lying tend to touch their nose is that it is likely to get itchy, making the individual more conscious of it. This fact might have inspired the story of Pinocchio, whose nose famously grew longer when he told a lie. Scientists in Chicago have found erectile tissue in the nose that is responsible for a slight engorgement of nasal tissue, which could arise either in the case of sexual arousal or due to a release of hormones triggered by lying. This inflammation would prompt an inclination to touch the nose more frequently.

Other 'tells'
Discomfort in liars may also be seen in a tendency to squirm in their seat, as though they would like to escape from the situation. The person who rubs their eyes while saying 'I see what you mean' may be saying that underneath he/she is refusing to accept the point. People who are lying tend to use fewer emphatic gestures, as though their hands are refusing to reinforce the subterfuge. On the other hand, there is an increase in their use of 'hand shrugs'. Waving a hand sideways may be a gesture emanating from some deeper part of the personality that is trying to disclaim

responsibility for the spoken lie. Effectively, the shrugging hand negates what is being said.

REMEMBER THIS!!! People who are lying tend to keep more of a physical distance from the other person and are more likely to turn away from the person they are addressing. Turning one shoulder towards the other person (a 'cold shoulder') is one postural indicator that all is not well with the situation. The feeling is that the liar is anticipating some form of retaliation should the lie be discovered and hence needs to keep their distance with defensive barriers in place.

Micro-expressions

Experts can detect signs of conflict indicating deception in a speaker by analysing tiny stress-induced twitches of the face, so fleeting that they cannot be seen at normal speed. Slowing down a video recording so that the face can be studied frame-by-frame reveals these micro-expressions, which take the form of little grimaces lasting just a fraction of a second. These represent 'counter emotions', suggesting that at some level the individual is uncomfortable with the lies they are telling. It is as though a higher brain centre is cancelling a mood expression that has been automatically initiated at a deeper level, effectively telling the face to 'shut up'.

When stakes are high

When a liar is under special pressure and it is very important that they are not rumbled, there are some particular features that may be observed. These include pupil dilation, raised voice pitch, shorter utterances and speech hesitations. Compared to less motivated liars, people who are trying very hard to avoid detection sometimes succeed in over-controlling gestures that they believe will give them away. For example, they contrive not to blink so often, keep their head and body very still and keep a fixed gaze on the person they are lying to.

This reveals a complex game of second-guessing and reveals how difficult it can be to detect liars. Because shifty-eyed people are widely thought of as untrustworthy, skilled liars may learn to override this signal and end up by exaggerating the amount of eye contact they use. Rather than glance away intermittently, they stare you straight in the face while delivering the lie. At the same time they may be taking pains to avoid blinking and squirming because these are widely believed to be tell-tale signs.

THINK ABOUT IT

The paradox is that publicity given to research on how to detect deceit can render those discoveries useless because people concentrate on overriding them. Ultimately, there comes a time when the *reverse* body language may be what we need to look out for (i.e. magnified 'honesty' signals such as an absence of blinking and squirming). Psychopaths may be especially good at controlling the leakage of deception.

Good and bad liars

Some people are certainly more skilled at lying than others. Actors and politicians are among those who are usually 'high self-monitors', always conscious of the impression they are making on others. Men tend to be better at concealing emotions than women (more 'poker-faced') but women tend to be better at reading body language (more 'intuitive'). It follows that women read other women best and men are particularly poor at detecting the real agenda of other men. There is some evidence that Oriental people can often read the emotions of Westerners better than their own ethnic group. Autistic individuals notoriously cannot read emotions in other people; show them a picture of someone laughing or crying and they have difficulty in saying what that person is feeling.

Tips on detecting liars

1. Emotions that appear on one side of the face only (asymmetrical), or which involve the mouth and not the upper part of the face, are more likely to be simulated than real. This is because different neural pathways are involved in consciously manufactured emotions as against those that are spontaneously felt.

2. Longer than usual pauses in a narrative and delays in answering a question may suggest lying. This often happens when a liar is unprepared for a question and needs time to concoct a plausible answer. Generally speaking, liars under questioning tend to slow down their account to give themselves time to think.

3. The pitch of the voice also denotes emotion. A person's voice tends to be higher when they are anxious or afraid and this may be due to an attempt to deceive. Stammering, voice tremors, mumbling and fumbling for words indicate stress, which is perhaps, in turn, caused by lying. (Note, however, that there are other causes of stress apart from lying that produce voice impediments, and that practised liars do not necessarily stammer.)

4. Tall stories often contain a paucity of detail, particularly when the storyteller is not highly imaginative or accomplished as a liar. Their concern is that any particular detail may be shown to be fabricated, providing solid evidence of untruth. Hence there is a tendency towards vagueness in an untruthful account of events.

5. A technique used by some interrogators when they believe they have been told a lie is to carry on the conversation for a while and then repeat the same question a bit later. The liar is likely to be rattled by this because it registers as a challenge and they have to rapidly recall exactly what they said previously.

6. Blushing may be a giveaway; most obviously it is pro-voked by embarrassment but it is also associated with a sense of shame or guilt and hence may suggest lying. The same applies to other signs of autonomic arousal, such as sweating, blinking, pupil dilation, increased swallowing and changes in breathing patterns. Of course, like voice tremors, these are general stress signs and there may be reasons for feeling stressed other than lying. Care should be taken not to discount these other possibilities.

7. Biting the lip and puckering of the mouth also suggest some kind of tension as though the individual is trying to intercept an inadvertent spilling of the truth they are trying to withhold.

8. The hand-shrug (waving a single hand outwards) may effectively discard what the person is saying as unrelia-ble. However, opening the palms symmetrically is more likely to be a sign of openness (having nothing to hide).

9. Attempts at deception are sometimes betrayed by what is *not* seen rather than what is observed. For example, if a person is recounting a traumatic experience, then the absence of distress signs (e.g. a tear in the corner of the eye or a crinkling of the brow) may be an indica-tion that they are not reliving an actual episode. When a person is expressing regret it is likely they are being

insincere if the sides of their mouth do not turn down symmetrically.

10. It should be recognised that some criminals and psychopaths never display guilt because they don't feel any. Their behaviour is consistent with their value system (it's just that their values differ from ours). In some instances this may even allow them to falsely pass a polygraph test. Others (innocent people) may sometimes fail a polygraph test because they know they are suspected and are afraid they may be incorrectly identified as guilty. The order of questioning is supposed to guard against 'false positives' of this sort but is not guaranteed to do so.

Famous liars

Kim Philby was a highly placed official in the British Secret Service until his defection to the Soviet Union confirmed suspicions that he was a Russian agent. After two of his colleagues (Burgess and Maclean) had previously defected, Philby appeared in a newsreel denying that he too was a traitor. Although he appeared superficially confident, slowing down the film revealed fleeting facial twitches indicative of stress. He also produced a rather silly, inappropriate grin when denying his guilt. This reflects an inner voice saying 'how embarrassing' or 'what a joke me sitting here and telling such porkies'. The same silly smile was seen in a Nottingham student who appeared on TV to appeal for the safe return of his missing girlfriend; it turned out he had murdered her and concealed her body under the floor-boards of her flat.

The Bill Clinton tapes have been studied particularly closely because they were readily accessible to body language analysts. When being quizzed about his affair he became tongue-tied and tended to break his gaze at critical points when pressure was high and he was grasping for a suitable response. He also showed inappropriate smiling and it was noted that he touched his nose rather frequently, a nose that was slightly bulbous at the best of times but perhaps further inflamed by the stress of having to lie. His high profile would have increased stress, but against that he may have been helped by being a skilled politician and probably persuaded himself that his particular sexual activities did not amount to a 'relationship' with Monica Lewinsky.

Tracie Andrews, a British woman who murdered her boyfriend and tried to blame it on an incident of road-rage, avoided eye contact with journalists who were interviewing her and repeatedly put her hand to her face. These 'leakages' are of course more obvious in retrospect than at the time, particularly since one is easily distracted in the live interview by the floods of tears and the words being said. It also helps to have a baseline for comparison, which is why police interviews, as well as polygraph tests, usually start with some innocuous questions that can be answered truthfully.

Some liars are very hard to spot. Ferdinand Demara, whose fame prompted the book and film called *The Great Imposter*, escaped exposure for many years during which he faked his college grades to get a commission in the navy, then added a PhD to his name to secure a post of Dean of Philosophy in a Canadian college. Next, he acquired some medical knowledge and with fraudulent credentials joined the Royal Canadian Navy medical service, where he carried out complex operations in Korea. He was ultimately exposed by a newspaper reporter and diagnosed as a psychopath. Like many liars, he got away with it for so long because people are not normally expecting outright deceit, especially in medical and academic circles.

How to conceal dishonesty

1. To be a successful liar, the best approach is that used by actors trained in the so-called 'method', which works from the inside out. It involves recalling an instance from one's past that would be expected to generate the emotion required in the current situation, whether it be distress, joy or anger, and running this scenario through the head while perpetrating the lie. In this way the emotion will be truly felt, and therefore be more convincing, even though it is really a 'transplant'.

2. It is a good idea to keep the fictional account as close to the truth as possible. This enables details to be discussed with minimal strain and there is less chance of

critical error or tension leakage. For example, everything about your movements on an evening in question might be true, except for the identity of the person you were with. Inventing an entirely new account adds extra mental load, which can be the giveaway to an expert lie detector (such as your spouse).

3. Since most liars give themselves away by movements of the body more than the face, it may be useful to position yourself in such a way that part of your body at least is concealed from the person you are talking to. This might be achieved, for example, by sitting behind a desk. Alternatively, you may contrive to be doing something active like making coffee or doing some photocopying at the same time. This will make it more difficult to pick up on the body movements that could betray deception.

IF YOU REMEMBER ONE THING It is worth remembering that most lies are ultimately unveiled, hence it is generally better to 'tell the truth and shame the devil'. Many people, especially intimate partners, can forgive almost anything except being lied to.

How to look trustworthy

Research on perception of trustworthiness shows that to some extent it is based on innate features. People with an upturned (U-shaped) mouth, wide-open eyes and distinct cheekbones are usually seen as more trustworthy. Generally, these are feminine, baby-faced features. Hyper-macho, dominant faces are generally less trusted, although being handsome does help. Advertisers also know that mature, silver-haired experts like Michael Parkinson and David Attenborough are among the most credible individuals when it comes to product endorsement.

There are certain ways to make ourselves appear more trustworthy, which of course overlap with the techniques for making people like us. Some major tips are as follows:

1. A smile is the most important single thing. It conveys the message 'you are safe' and 'all is well'. Of course, it helps if the smile appears genuine. The genuine smile comes on slowly, spends only a short time at its peak, and fades away slowly. As noted above, it also appears as crinkling around the eyes as well as lifting of the outsides of the mouth. This is the ideal; however, even a smile that is not truly felt is better than a totally expressionless face when it comes to engendering trust.

2. Avoid pursing the lips. This conveys either tension or an attempt to appear shrewd – either way it does not go down well.

3. Raise your eyebrows. This opens up the eyes and makes you look more open generally, whereas squinting makes us look slightly sinister. However, the elevation of the

eyebrows needs to be relaxed and confident; excessive furrowing of the brow comes over as stormy and troubled.

4. Opening the palms conveys the message that you have nothing to hide and can therefore be trusted.

5. Avoid barrier signals such as folding your arms, clutching things to your chest, covering your face with your hands or blowing smoke in the other person's face.

6. Mirror the posture and gestures of the person you are talking to. This will put them at ease because you are showing that you are 'just like them'.

7. Know what you are going to say and deliver it with conviction and enthusiasm. Use an average tempo (neither a drawl nor a machine-gun) and minimise throat clearings, long empty pauses and repetitive phrases. Such things are distracting and reduce credibility.

Computerised lie detection

We have probably evolved to be gullible to some extent, since little white lies are essential to the normal functioning of society. Unfortunately, this makes us susceptible to bigger lies on other occasions. Whatever cues are used by Dr Lightman to spot liars can be programmed into computers. In fact, computers have the potential to be more effective than humans as lie detectors because they can work simultaneously with a full array of cues, including those too fleeting for humans to register. They can also focus more easily on body language cues without being distracted by what is being said.

The full spectrum of insincerity indicators may be programmed, such that when people are attempting deception (e.g. when going through customs or immigration, or being questioned at a police station) this could be flagged up electronically. Voice stress analysis and infrared (heat) cameras, which show heat distribution around the face and neck, are already being used for this purpose. This is likely to be the future of lie detection and it will no doubt be increasingly difficult for fibbers to get away with their fiction.

6. My space or yours?

It's a three-dimensional world, and the physical distance between people – and the way they are oriented when interacting – tells us a great deal about how much they like each other and the dominance relationships among them. Knowing the 'rules' of distance and positioning (sometimes called 'proxemics') can help us recognise what effect we are having on other people and in understanding their attitude towards us.

Generally speaking, we stand closer to people and turn our body in their direction when we are positively disposed towards them. In a sexually charged situation this might imply flirting. When we dislike somebody, or want to escape their company, we back off and turn away.

Personal space
For any given interaction between two people there is a socially prescribed ideal distance between them that strikes the balance between warmth and threat. Within about 18 inches of our body is an 'intimate zone' usually reserved for lovers, spouses, our children and close family members. At this distance we can touch them, smell their body odours and see pores and blemishes in their complexion. Only in exceptional circumstances (like contact sports, concerts and public transport) is it acceptable to get this close to people with whom we are not on intimate terms.

Most of our conversations with friends and acquaintances takes place at a distance of between 18 inches and 4 feet. This is the 'social or friendship zone'. Occasional, non-intimate touching may occur, e.g. for purposes of greeting, congratulation or reassurance. More formal social and business interactions occur at a distance of about 4–9 feet (the 'business zone'). At this distance touching is not possible, except for shaking hands, which requires both parties to stretch out a hand in order to bridge the gap. Lectures and conversations with very important people employ distances of more than 9 feet. This is called the 'public zone'.

Social distance

Differences in social rank are reflected in physical differences between people. An ordinary person stays further away from royalty, or even their boss, than they do from their own peers. This is why we may regard those who keep their distance from us as self-opinionated snobs, while those who get uncomfortably close are seen as pushy and presumptuous. Maintaining the 'correct' distance from another person is an important social skill that needs to be acquired or others will be offended.

If someone gets inappropriately close and we feel that our space is being violated, we attempt to compensate, usually by backing away. If physical withdrawal is not possible, as in a lift or crowded tube train, we control intimacy by any other means that is at our disposal. We may turn away or avoid eye contact, and if conversation occurs at all, it will usually be restricted to safe topics such as the weather or non-threatening, jokey observations. Intrusive questions such as 'Where do you live?' or 'Are you married?' are particularly taboo in conditions of enforced physical intimacy.

Space invasion

Next time you are in a social situation such as a party and talking with a stranger, try getting within their intimate zone (say about 10–12 inches away from them) and make eye contact. The chances are that, however they perceive your motive, they will back off so as to 'correct' the distance between you back to the social norm. If you then close the gap again, they will back off again, and you may find yourself effectively chasing them around the room. At some point, they are likely to feel so uncomfortable that they will find an excuse to leave your company altogether and go off to talk with someone else. You may then want to explain to them what you were up to and hope that they regard it as a talking point. Obviously, it is best not to experiment on someone you might have wanted to impress.

Cultural differences

There are noticeable differences across cultures in the accepted use of social space. Latin Americans and Middle Eastern people accept closer proximity and more touching than Anglo-Americans, while the English are even more standoffish. Since closeness is a marker of liking, the English tend to misunderstand people of other cultures as being over-familiar, while those others think of the English as cold. However, this is simply down to the attempts of each group to attain what to them is a comfortable distance.

Sex differences also have to be considered. Women are inclined to get closer to intimate friends than are men but prefer even greater distances from strangers. Men are less affected by the nature of their relationship but usually like to maintain a greater distance from other men than from women.

Personality differences also apply; extraverts are happier in crowded conditions than are introverts.

Erecting barriers

When we dislike or distrust others around us we tend to erect barriers to defend our personal space. For example, a person who feels threatened or exposed may arrange their hands across the front of their body as though to protect it. This may mean simply folding their arms across their chest, or the creation of the barrier may be deflected or disguised as a small grooming action such as straightening one's tie or adjusting the cuffs.

Even powerful and experienced public figures like Prince Charles may feel the need for a defensive ritual when venturing into new territory. A dignitary who is just arriving in a foreign country (off a plane or ship) is more likely to perform checking operations that take the hands in front of their body than are those receiving them as visitors – and the same applies to ordinary people. This stems from the fact that the visitor is off their own ground and thus feeling vulnerable.

Physical objects may also be used as barriers. The man who sits behind a large desk is effectively saying 'Look how important I am'. At the same time he is ensuring that visitors to his office cannot approach him too closely. Similarly, the speaker who prefers to remain on an elevated stage, keeping a lectern between himself and the audience, is either using spatial language to emphasise the status difference between himself and the audience, or is insecure in some way about himself or how his message will be received.

Defending our space

People occupy and defend space in much the same way that tribes and nations do. This can be observed whenever people are gathered together in public, in parks, on streets, on beaches or at parties. Observe a line of people waiting for service at a bank or post office. They behave as though there is an invisible bubble surrounding each person that gives rise to even spacing between them. Each individual respects the personal space of those nearby. A three-dimensional equivalent can be observed on a crowded beach in summer, when each newly arriving family selects an area of sand to set up camp that is as far removed from other sunbathers as possible. If someone gets unnecessarily close they had better have a good reason or they will be viewed with suspicion. (Even more suspect is the man who takes his position at a urinal right next to another man when there are plenty of other options.)

Within this context of roughly even distribution, dominant people lay claim to greater amounts of territory and are inclined to expand it at the expense of others. Body space may be extended in a variety of ways: putting one's name on the door, establishing a favourite chair that strategically commands a room, putting articles of clothing or books on chairs, erecting partitions (even if only moving a plant towards the person at the desk next door). If informal agreement cannot be reached, arguments and actual fights may ensue. Raised to a national scale, this is a major cause of wars.

The sunlounger syndrome

Some people on holiday get up early in the morning to 'reserve' their favourite sunlounger by placing a towel on it. The same territorial behaviour can be seen in many other contexts. Try leaving a

98

coat or a bag on a public seat in a fairly crowded room then stand back and watch. Most people are hesitant to move an article that has been left on a seat, even if the person who left it is not around and has no right to reserve a seat in this way. Some may look at the article and think about it, but only a very brave individual will ask if it belongs to anyone before moving it aside so they can sit down.

On whose territory?

The assumption (and acceptance) of dominance is greater when a person is on their own territory. Other things being equal, an incumbent can be dislodged only if the usurper is unmistakably more powerful. Even low-ranked persons can behave with great bravery, confidence and determination when operating from their own home or workspace. This is why bosses prefer to call employees into their office to interview them or give them a dressing down, rather than going to see them in their own workspace.

If a man comes home to find his wife in bed with a lover, the lover will usually retreat, even if he is bigger or higher in social rank. This may be partly down to guilt but it is also in recognition of the fact that people fight more ferociously in defence of their own patch than when they are away from home.

The 'home and away' effect is well known in sports circles and has deep instinctive well-springs that go way beyond the expectation of social support on one's home ground.

When a business meeting is arranged it is usually held on the ground of the socially dominant party. However, the warmth of the greeting is indicated by the extent to which the greeter 'puts himself out'. Does he, for example, go to the airport to meet his guest, come out onto the doorstep to shake his hand, or just remain at his desk and have the visitor shown in to him? The more trouble the visitor has in reaching the host the more belittled he is.

Body pointing

The way in which a person's body is oriented tells us much about the direction in which he/she would like to go. If you are standing at a party talking to someone and their feet (hence much of their body) are pointing outward and past you, the chances are they have plans to move on. Perhaps they find you boring or perhaps there is someone else they are particularly keen to meet. They may just be desperate to go to the bathroom or refill their glass. For whatever reason, they are trying to keep the conversation open in order to escape when an opportunity arises.

It is not uncommon for strangers to stand in such a way that their bodies form an approximate right-angle. If this is mutual it signals a low to moderate level of intimacy and allows for others to join in the conversation. So long as there is mirroring of gestures there is no necessary strain in this open formation but the conversation will probably stay light and informal. When privacy is sought the formation is closed into a face-to-face position and the distance between the two parties is decreased. However, at this point one or the other may show signs of wanting to escape from the situation. This can be detected by foot and body pointers and glances in other directions seeking rescue.

If a third party attempts to join a pair who are in the closed formation the established pair can either accept the newcomer by opening up and turning their bodies towards them, or effectively freeze them out by turning their heads only. At some point the excluded individual will usually move off to avoid embarrassment.

When two men compete for one woman, the first sign of her preference may be seen in the fact that her feet will point towards one rather than the other, thus beginning the process of exclusion.

Body orientation also works when people are seated. If three people are seated on a sofa, the one in the middle has the power to choose whether to interact primarily to the left or to the right. Depending on the way he/she crosses their legs, the body will be naturally inclined towards one and a barrier set against the other. The only way the excluded individual can effectively re-enter the social exchange is to bring a single chair round to the front of the other two – but this may come across as rather desperate.

Seating arrangements

The way in which people choose their seating positions socially and at work tells us much about the roles they are likely to adopt. Intimate couples usually sit side-by-side, but crowded restaurants and bars do not always permit this formation and the couple may be forced to sit opposite one another. There are also sex differences in this respect. Women tend to prefer the side-by-side position with their partner, because it permits touching, whereas men usually choose to sit and face their partner across a table, so that they can look at them more easily. This is not intended to be confrontational so much as territorial: it closes others out.

In an office meeting situation, the person who sits beside another tends to have a cooperative attitude towards that person. The one who sits opposite is more likely to be competitive or defensive. One who sits on a near corner is fairly neutral, while the one who chooses a distant corner is independent or uninterested (or simply wants to get away early). If a table is rectangular, the most powerful position is at the head of the table at the end furthest from the door, near to the blackboard. It would be presumptuous of anyone other than the chairperson or boss to take this place. In a relatively democratic organisation, however, the person chairing the meeting may take the middle of one long side of the table (away from the entrance door). This makes for better communication with all of the others around the table. Others take their place around the boss accordingly. The second most powerful person in the organisation is likely to sit on the right of the boss (his/her 'right hand man') while the one who compiles the minutes usually sits on the left.

 As already noted, a table between two people operates as a barrier. There may be specific reasons for sitting opposite one another – for example, a boss is reprimanding a worker, or an employee wants to signal acceptance of the boss's superior status. However, friendly contact is much more easily made in the cooperative or neutral positions mentioned above. Conversations are usually shorter and less formal when conducted in this way, and negotiation is facilitated.

When two people sit directly opposite one another an invisible line through the middle of the table marks out their territory. If a salesperson presents a sample to a potential buyer, the buyer may either lean across the table to look at it or take it back into their own territory. Only in the latter instance does the salesperson have non-verbal permission to enter the other's territory by realigning themselves into the cooperative position (alongside them). If the sample is pushed back across the table before the salesperson has relocated, it is probably going to be ultimately rejected.

Not all tables are rectangular. King Arthur was famed for adopting a round table to indicate that all his knights had equal status. However, things are not that simple, because wherever Arthur sat would have become the head of the table, so those knights closest to him (especially on his right) would have been ranked next, and the one opposite would be cast in the competitive/defensive position. Despite this, round tables are less formal than rectangular ones and hence preferred for coffee and relaxed meetings in offices. If space permits, a round dining table in the home engenders a more open, less authoritarian atmosphere.

Tips on how to put someone at ease

When you have a visitor who is off their own territory they are likely to feel some degree of insecurity. If you wish to put them at their ease, whether for business, social or romantic purposes, the following tips might be useful:

1. Choose a low-level table (preferably round or oval shaped), and place it in a nice cosy corner, perhaps with a plant beside it.

2. Have them sit with their back to a wall or room partition and away from open doors and windows. This way they have no fear (conscious or subconscious) of anyone approaching from behind. This promotes general

physiological relaxation and consequently makes them more amenable.

3. Seat yourself at a 45-degree angle to them, rather than right beside them or directly opposite. This gives the feeling that you will be cooperating on a mutual task.

4. Be sure that no barriers, such as a briefcase on the table, are separating you.

5. Avoid folding your arms and, if you cross your legs at all, bring the outer leg over the top so your body is turned towards them.

6. Soft lights, music, and an open fire also relax people, so that a more favourable response can be expected to your proposition.

7. Most important of all, offer a drink of some kind, making it clear that it doesn't have to be alcoholic, and provide some food to share, even if it's just nibbles. (Food-sharing is a basic way of welcoming others into our 'tribe'. In the Pacific, the drinking of *kava* has important bonding significance. Among native Americans, it's the peace-pipe, while hippies share joints and bongs. Any slight intoxication provided by these activities could be a bonus.)

7. Make your presence felt

There is an amusing scene in Charlie Chaplin's film *The Great Dictator* in which Hitler prepares for a vital first meeting with Mussolini. Hitler's advisors have sought to gain advantage by seating him on a high platform behind a very large desk, with a very much smaller and lower chair for Mussolini to sit on. The plan is that Il Duce should enter through doors at the lower end of the hall and have to walk a long, exposed distance up to Der Führer, who will be waiting behind his desk up on the stage. A stern bust of Hitler has been placed on the desktop so that, even if he himself is smiling, his image will still be glaring across the desk to intimidate his rival.

In the event, Mussolini confounds all these preparations by appearing from a door on the stage behind Hitler's chair. He quickly establishes dominance by towering over him, slapping him on the back in a familiar and patronising way, and striking a match on the back of the bust (which is now pointing harmlessly away from him) in order to light a cigar and blow smoke in the Führer's face.

Although presented as comedy, this exchange typifies the kind of jockeying for position that goes on between people (men especially) all the time, whether in professional politics or everyday life. For the most part it occurs spontaneously and unconsciously, but if we are aware of the principles involved we are better placed to assert ourselves and avoid being put upon by others. Note that many of the rules of spatial advantage described in the previous chapter were being used in this example. Bosses use a formidable desk in order to say 'Look how important I am' as well as placing barriers to prevent visitors to their office approaching too closely.

Who is boss?

Dominance is partly predetermined according to the social position held by an individual. If they are the appointed director or teacher, or have socially prescribed rank of some kind, then there may be little one can do to alter the hierarchy. However, power relationships are seldom set in stone and some people emit signals that help them gain ascendancy over others.

In the animal world one of the most obvious bases of dominance is physical size. Especially among males (usually the more competitive sex), large individuals tend to rise in the hierarchy more easily than smaller ones. They may have to pump themselves up somehow and appear threatening in order to achieve this, or the dominance may be simply granted.

It is no accident that in the majority of presidential contests in the US the taller candidate has usually won. Similarly, a study published in the *Wall Street Journal* found that men over 6ft 2ins in height had salaries that were 12% higher than those of men under 6ft tall.

Wildlife experts recommend that if confronted by a bear in the forest the worst thing you can do is turn and run; the advice is to backtrack slowly, while at the same time making yourself look as big as possible, for example by extending your arms widely like semaphore signals. At the human level, clothes may help us to appear big, for example with shoulder pads, copious robes or a large hat (think of the Pope and his cardinals with their shovel hats, or Isambard Kingdom Brunel with his trademark tall top hat).

Spreading oneself wide

Even if you are not naturally very big it is possible to create the appearance of size by sprawling one's limbs so as to occupy as much space as possible. The boss of a company is likely to lean backwards in their chair, stretch their legs out in front of them as far as possible and place their hands on the back of their head so their elbows are spread as triangles on each side.

Although people who make a large spatial impact are seen as dominant, it does not necessarily follow that employees should respond by echoing such a posture. Mirroring can be flattering and friendly in some circumstances but sprawling in one's chair is more likely to come across as disrespectful, or even as challenging to the boss's authority.

 Unsuccessful challenges to the boss's authority are certain to leave you worse off. The general advice is never to challenge someone unless you are certain to win.

Generally speaking, dominant people are able to relax while submissive ones need to be attentive. For example, subordinates may be required to rise when a high-ranking person enters the room. People who are self-assured and confident of their status sit casually, while those of lower status sit upright, fold their knees together, tuck their hands neatly in their lap, and fold one foot behind the other, creating a 'pretzel' effect. Departures from this social rule that are intended to renegotiate relative status have to be managed very judiciously if they are not to cause offence and end up as counter-productive.

Showing due respect

Since the body language of dominance derives largely from apparent size, it follows that signals of submission are those that render the individual smaller. This is the reason why the 'pretzel' posture comes across as timid. Bowing, curtseying, kneeling, or lying on the ground face down (as required by the Siamese courtiers in *The King and I*) are even more obvious examples of making oneself smaller. They convey the message, 'Don't attack me, I am already down'. The posture adopted in prayer, especially by Muslims, is obviously one of submission. Doffing the cap is a ritual form of showing respect by lifting one's hat entirely off the head (so as not to look taller than one really is).

Such postures have the same meaning anywhere in the world, although the details of how and when they are performed is modified by etiquette. In Japan, the precise depth to which one bows when greeting someone is of great importance because it denotes proper respect for the social status of the other person. Recognition of this means that when Westerners meet Japanese people, both tend to exaggerate their bow just to be on the safe side, sometimes to the point of seeming ridiculous.

It is a matter of royal protocol that nobody is supposed to touch the Queen of England. This was famously violated by Australia's prime minister John Keating who, in 1992, was photographed putting his hand around the Queen's back in order to guide her in a particular direction. Although he denied that physical contact occurred, the British tabloids were outraged and dubbed him the 'Lizard of Oz'.

This act of over-familiarity was trumped in 2012 when the new Australian premier Julia Gillard placed a guiding hand on the backside of President Obama when he was making a state visit. He was seen awkwardly restraining her with his own hand. The problem arises when an incumbent leader, being on their own territory, assumes social dominance which is not recognised by a high-status visitor who is unused to being patronised.

Shake on it

The handshake in Western society is a greeting gesture with similar significance to the Japanese bow and it is equally important to get it right. The person who is in the socially dominant position, either because of their official status or the assertive nature of their personality, is usually the one to initiate the handshake, offering their hand first (although there is a convention that a woman should first offer to shake hands with a man). Thereafter, dominance is demonstrated by the strength of their grip and the angle of the palm. The dominant individual tends to turn his or her hand over the top of the other person's hand, rather in the manner of a hand-wrestler.

Once again some subtlety is necessary. Nobody is impressed by a handshake that feels like a dead fish, but nor do they enjoy having their fingers crushed by someone trying to prove how macho they are. A balance needs to be struck between impotence and aggressiveness. The ideal is a firm but measured grip that is sensitive to the occasion and the relationship as it really is.

 There are some possible ways of countering an overly assertive handshake. One is to put your spare (left) hand over the back of the other person's hand. Another is to step towards the other person in such a way as to invade their territory. However, there is a danger of turning a simple greeting into something approximating to war. It should be remembered that true dominance, like true love, is something given rather than taken by force.

A variation on the standard handshake is for one of the participants to bring their left hand into play by placing it somewhere on the arm anywhere up to the shoulder. This is perhaps more often seen in the US than the UK and is associated with extravert, self-confident people who want to express a special desire to be friendly. While genuine warmth may be conveyed in this way, there is a danger that it can come across as insincere and slightly patronising, especially since politicians and high-pressure salespersons are often seen to use it.

Who are you looking at?
The issue of who is allowed to look at whom is of particular significance in some cultural contexts. In gang culture, merely looking at another person may be seen as an

intrusion that evokes aggression. Bowing not only makes us lower than the person we are showing respect to, but by lowering the head it also makes us less threatening by turning our gaze to the floor. Even a nod of appreciation to another person is a residual of the same tendency to turn our eyes downwards in the presence of a high-status person.

Staring someone down

If you are feeling adventurous you might try staring at a stranger in a waiting room or on public transport. They will attempt to break contact by looking away but if they find that you are continuing to gaze at them they will begin to feel uncomfortable and might move away from you because they see you as dangerous. (Caution: don't try this when you are trying to impress someone or if they look as though they might actually be dangerous.)

Taking a stance

The way in which people stand tells us much about their attitude. The cowboy stance, with legs spread, hands on hips, thumbs tucked into the belt, and shoulders thrown backwards, is a dominance display that is used particularly by men who are trying to look tough to other men or virile to women. Standing with legs wide apart is what one does on public transport to avoid being thrown off balance

– hence the same posture, with feet firmly planted on the ground, transmits the message that one is not going anywhere. An increasing number of women also adopt this aggressive stance as either flirtation or a challenge, or as some mixture of both.

 When two men confront each other in this way the angle of their feet may be critical. If their toes point directly towards each other there is likely to be trouble. Turning one foot outwards swivels the body slightly and will help to defuse an otherwise dangerous situation. We have already noted that feet position may also be a signal as to whether others are welcome to join in a conversation. If people stand with their feet at right-angles, others are not excluded; but if they are turned 'full frontal', others are effectively frozen out.

When people are standing at a function with others they do not know well, they tend to adopt a defensive posture. They stand at a greater distance than they would with close friends and cross their arms and legs, often shielding their genitals with their hands. As they relax in each other's company, their closed posture gives way to a more open one. Ankles are uncrossed and the hands are used more for gesturing than defence, with wrists and palms exposed in a friendly way. The feet then point towards the people they find most interesting and they may even venture to touch each other.

Leaning on a wall may be a sign of relaxation but standing in a doorway with one hand outstretched on the door jamb is territorial and slightly intimidatory. If this message is intentional then well and good, but some people create a bad impression by adopting this domineering pose habitually. In this case they should practise putting their hands by their sides and showing their palms from time to time to soften their stance.

Assertiveness is not anger

Anger may be used as a threat display in that its expression is the residual of a threat to attack. Pulling the brow over the eyes in a frown, clenching the teeth and fists, and thrusting the head forward are preparations for fighting and hence express anger. This may frighten a rival away but is unlikely to impress them otherwise.

THINK ABOUT IT

As noted above, it is a paradox of dominance that it is largely granted by the submissive party rather than taken by force. Animals at the top of their hierarchy seldom have to fight other members of their group, and those further down seldom improve their position by scrapping with those above them. Even measured in terms of the biochemistry of hormones, dominance is virtually the opposite of hostility.

Dominance is also partly specific to a situation. One person may be boss at work because he or she owns the company but another may be dominant in the local operatic society because they are a better singer and get the plum parts. And of course when people are on their home territory they have an advantage.

People who stand up for their rights in an insistent, yet calm and reasonable way are most likely to improve their situation. This is what assertiveness training seeks to achieve. The person who loses their temper almost certainly loses the argument into the bargain; all he or she does is arouse resentment and resistance in the other.

People who talk in loud voices are also seldom dominant; rather they may have learned that they have to speak up or nobody will listen to them. A quiet voice like that used by Marlon Brando in *The Godfather* is usually a great deal more menacing. If the initial hurdle of persuading people to hush so they can hear what is being said is successfully negotiated, then a certain amount of power has been exercised already. The ideal, according to Theodore Roosevelt, is 'speak softly and carry a big stick'.

How to get ahead

Is it possible to gain dominance by conscious alteration and control of our body language? It may sometimes help, provided that the manufactured power signals are not grossly out of step with people's socially assigned status. In that case there is a risk of simply appearing rude and insulting, and you might be thoroughly 'brought down to size'.

Slapping the boss on the back in an over-familiar way, or intruding on their space by putting your feet up on their desk, is unlikely to benefit you as an employee. However, there are circumstances when the hierarchy is not a clearly established 'given', in which case some degree of dominance play could be advantageous. For example, when mixing with other people in a social group such as a cocktail partly, where people are perhaps meeting for the first time, it may be helpful to contrive dominant body language (relaxation, self-confidence, bodily expansiveness, etc.).

There are other circumstances in which a display of submissiveness can be more helpful than generating power signals. When the driver of a car you have just bumped into is both very big and very angry, survival may depend on eating a bit of humble pie (regardless of who is technically in the right). When a traffic police officer has stopped you for a violation, a certain show of humility and a polite apology may help to avoid a ticket. Sales staff are often taught that coming around from behind a desk or counter may defuse the aggression of an irate customer. Women are particularly skilled in the judicious use of submissive, vulnerable signals to gain the cooperation and help of others, and are thus often better negotiators.

The 'anchoring' trick
The approach to behavioural analysis called 'neurolinguistic programming' recommends a number of special techniques for influencing others. One particular gimmick is called **anchoring**. For example, a salesperson encourages a client to talk about something enjoyable and close to their heart, such as a pet, a sport or hobby. They then 'anchor' this feeling with a small action such as a cough or sneeze. Later on, when the conversation has turned to the product that is being sold, this same anchor is reintroduced to revive the positive association. Although many people would regard this kind of manipulation as unethical, it may be a successful way of getting someone on-side with whatever you are 'selling'.

Seven ways to look impressive

Although it is not always advantageous to appear dominant, it is possible to contrive this appearance if desired. The following are a few things that could be tried:

1. Leaning backwards on the balls of the feet as you walk tilts your head and body upwards and gives the impression of self-confidence.

2. Be expansive. Occupying a large amount of space is a major way to appear dominant. Spreading one's arms and legs akimbo is the easiest way of achieving this,

and it applies whether one is standing, sitting down or moving about. It can also be achieved by surrounding yourself with objects like books or an umbrella.

3. Avoid fidgeting. Powerful people come across as self-confident and relaxed, as though they do not care what others think about them. This might mean leaning back in one's chair and putting one's hands behind the head. Even minor forms of anti-social behaviour like putting one's feet up on a chair can signal that one has no fear of consequences. Sitting rigidly in a chair with a tense neck and hands tucked into the lap has the reverse effect.

4. Form a 'steeple' with your hands under your chin. This comes across as a sign of authority because it suggests that a major decision is being conjured.

5. Lower your eyebrows so that your eyes are almost closed into a frown. (When eyebrows are raised high on the head one appears startled and infantile.)

6. Avoid gratuitous smiling. Serious faces are seen as more masculine and dominant than those that are smiling. This is because a smile is often viewed as placatory. Women are nearly always photographed smiling in the media, whereas political and business leaders, regardless of gender, are more often serious-faced. Research shows that high-testosterone individuals (whether male

or female) are less concerned about being friendly and hence smile less often.

7. Lower the pitch of your voice and talk quietly, slowly and deliberately. This is particularly important in a situation where one is seeking to be influential, such as returning unsatisfactory goods to a shop. Margaret Thatcher was supposedly taught how to do this in her early days as Conservative Party leader.

Dead Ringers

In the David Cronenberg film *Dead Ringers*, actor Jeremy Irons had the task of portraying a pair of identical twins, one of whom was outgoing and dominant and the other introvert and submissive. Anyone seeing the film will attest to his success in depicting a striking personality difference between the two characters. Irons later revealed that he had achieved the transformation between the two characters using a single 'switch'. The dominant twin walked on his heels, giving him an upright, expansive demeanour, while the submissive one walked on his toes, causing him to lean forward apologetically. This effect can easily be observed by walking in these two different styles past a floor-length mirror.

---

8. Sex magnets

According to Woody Allen, 'only two things in life are important: one is sex, and the other isn't all that important'. This is a view shared by most evolutionary psychologists, who argue that the key human motive is the 'sexual imperative', the need to pass our genes on to the following generation. Genes that do not succeed in reproducing themselves are lost for ever. Everything else, including our survival instinct, is subservient to this central aim.

Our first task is to attract a mate who is good breeding material. This translates into one who is sexually appealing. What makes people pretty, handsome and sexy is best understood by looking at how these characteristics have evolved.

What is sexy?

Think of someone you find devastatingly attractive – a film star, model or perhaps your current partner. List some of the primary attributes that make them appealing to you, first the physical, then the personality traits. Keep this list to hand as you read through the account that follows to see what rings a bell.

Three keys to beauty

Evolutionary psychologists have discovered that facial beauty depends on signals of reproductive fitness. In other words, both men and women look for markers of fertility and good parent potential in each other. Primary among these are:

1. **Averageness**: When photos of several faces of persons of the same gender are superimposed on each other, the composites appear as attractive. This is partly because blemishes and abnormalities are cancelled and the skin appears smooth, hence healthy, but also because average faces signal out-breeding, which has advantages for the breadth of immunity imparted to one's offspring.

2. **Symmetry**: Most people's faces are slightly different on the left and right sides. Those with more symmetrical faces are judged more attractive as mates. Symmetry implies 'developmental stability', meaning a history of resistance to stressors such as mutations, parasites and toxins. The partners of symmetrical men are reported to have more orgasms, presumably because the men are more desirable.

3. **Exaggerated gender**: While average female faces are attractive to men, they are even more attractive when female-typical traits are exaggerated. These are the things emphasised by make-up (bigger eyes, narrower

eyebrows, pinker complexion, fuller, redder lips, etc.). They are usually the attributes of young, mature women of around 24 years old, although some are younger still (e.g. the ideal lips are those typical of a 14-year-old girl). Blonde hair is preferred by many men because, like blue eyes, it is a trait associated with babies.

Baby-doll features are prized in women because they are most fertile when young. Smooth, pinkish skin, large open eyes, full lips and a small chin have apparently evolved in women to evoke parental protection from men. Pop songs refer to adult women as 'baby'; many people also use the word 'babe'. While women have borrowed baby signals, the breeding potential of men is much less age-dependent. Toyboys do exist (ask Mrs Robinson) but they are rarer and seldom long-lasting as partners.

THINK ABOUT IT Not surprisingly, composites of the faces of professional female models are more attractive than those based on ordinary women. Since average, symmetrical and female-exaggerated facial traits are oestrogen markers, composites of women high in oestrogen are also judged by men as more desirable than those of women low in oestrogen.

When it comes to choosing men, women are more complicated. Sometimes they like a manly (high-testosterone) face; at other times they prefer a softer look. Slightly feminised male faces (smaller chin, wider lips, larger eyes and higher arched eyebrows) are often judged by women as more attractive, presumably because they suggest personality characteristics, like empathy and reliability, that might make for good parenting. Fossil records suggest that male–female differences in humans have diminished over the last 100,000 years, presumably as a result of a female preference for caring men.

Women's preferences are cyclic

Whether a woman prefers a man who is macho or baby-faced, genetically similar or not, depends to some extent on whether she is in long-term or short-term mating mode. There is a shift towards a preference for 'macho' men, and those less closely related, when a woman is in mid-cycle, not pregnant, not on the contraceptive pill, and when she is having an affair. In other words, women seek 'good genes' when fertile; otherwise they favour 'resource provision'. (Research shows that use of the contraceptive pill largely eliminates the cyclic changes in female mate preference.)

A similar principle applies to reactions to dilated eye pupils. Dilated pupils are generally attractive because they make the eyes look bigger and because they give the impression that the other person is interested in us. This helps make a candle-lit dinner romantic – pupils are initially enlarged because the light is dim, but this is instinctively read by the partner across the table as emotional arousal, thus setting up a spiral of mutual desire.

Where men are concerned, the larger a woman's pupils the better. For women, large pupils are preferred only when they are mid-cycle, not on the pill, and are the type that likes 'bad boys' (indicating a short-term mating mode). When a long-term mate is sought, women prefer medium-sized pupils because the male partner is seen as better parent potential.

Body versus face

Which is more important in determining physical attractiveness, the body or the face? When models are rated separately with respect to body and face, the face is the better predictor of overall attractiveness. However, the body component assumes greater importance when men are assessing women for short-term affairs as against long-term relationships. No such shift occurs when women evaluate men. It is hence not surprising that women regard wandering eyes as a bad sign in a man.

Males are more excited by female beauty than vice versa. Brain responses are generally greater when people view attractive, relative to unattractive, faces but the difference is greater for men. This confirms the idea that, where sexual matters are concerned, men are more visual animals than women. However, women differentiate more than men with respect to the smell of potential partners, because this gives clues as to the nature of their immune system.

What is sex appeal?

Sex appeal is not exactly the same as beauty and is rather more complex. By and large, sex appeal derives from sexual dimorphism (the typical differences between men and women). For example, men find an hourglass figure attractive in women, while women like a V-shaped torso in men. Greater height and depth of voice is sexy in men, as is their 'musky' smell (contrasting with the relatively 'sweet' smell of women). These are markers of sex hormones, especially oestrogen versus testosterone, and they attract the opposite sex because they signal reproductive fitness.

 A key marker of fertility, hence sex appeal, in women is the waist/hip ratio. Low ratios, with the waist much narrower than the hips (ideally .7 to .8) are attractive to men because they indicate high oestrogen. By corollary, a tight, compact backside in a man is preferred by women because it signals testosterone. Women also often prefer this in themselves, giving rise to the clichéd concern about whether their 'bum looks big in this'. Perhaps women with this concern would be more reassured by reading some evolutionary psychology rather than reading women's magazines or soliciting their partner's opinion.

Innate releasers

Ethologists (scientists who study animal instincts) have shown that all species are equipped with certain 'innate releasing mechanisms'. These are stimulus patterns primed through evolution to evoke behaviour of survival importance. For example, humans readily acquire a fear of snakes and spiders because they were dangerous to our ancestors. In contrast, we fear cars much less than we should because they did not exist when our instincts were evolved.

The human male has an inborn tendency to be sexually excited by paired, pink, fleshy hemispheres. Anthropologist Desmond Morris has argued that breasts excite men because they 'echo' the rear presentation signal that is the key target for the human male. Support for such an idea comes from observation of certain primates, such as the gelada baboon, in which the female has copied her rear configuration onto her front side for purposes of sexual titillation and appeasement.

The role of imprinting

Such innate visual templates are subject to modification and consolidation in early childhood, according to what is actually encountered in the environment. This is called **imprinting**, and it accounts for some cultural variability as well as attachments to inappropriate targets that we call fetishism. Fetish objects are not determined by random conditioning; they nearly always have a strong sensory or symbolic association with the innate releaser. For example, a black high-heeled shoe is roughly the shape, colour and size of the pubic triangle. It traps pheromones after being worn, and has dominant, adult female connotations. Not surprisingly, shoe fetishists are more common than lawn-mower fetishists. Shoe fetishists are also more common than hat fetishists, probably because shoes are more prominent in the sightline of a crawling infant than hats (infancy being the time when fetishes are established).

Sexual displays

Both men and women display their attributes in order to attract mates. Nightclubs operate as human 'leks' (sexual display grounds like those used by colourful birds). Observations of people going in and out of nightclubs show that 50% more people leave as couples than arrive together.

Males approach females in nightclubs in accordance with the tightness of their clothes, the amount of flesh they expose (especially in the breast area) and the provocativeness of their dancing. These, in turn, vary with the phase of their cycle. When fertile, women tend to wear sexier clothes, display more flesh and dance more provocatively. The most successful females display at least 40% of their body and 50% of their breast area. The limit of exposure is the point where 'allure' transforms into concerns about promiscuity, which might signal other risk factors, or might be off-putting to someone looking for a long-term partner. Women seem to choose among the males who are brave (dominant) enough to ask them to dance.

 Male displays focus on demonstrating power and achievement. Research has found that a man seated in a Bentley Continental is seen as more attractive by women than the same man in a Ford Fiesta. By contrast, men are little influenced by status manipulations in their judgements of women. However, men do seem to recognise when they are impressing women; their testosterone (preparation for mating) increases after driving a Porsche in public and decreases after driving a banger.

Clearly, wealth and status are more important markers of 'mate value' to women than physical good looks. Body-builders are usually seen by women as self-absorbed narcissists, whereas intelligence, creativity, sense of humour and generosity (willingness to share resources) are highly rated by women.

Are the best men already taken?
It is widely supposed that eligibility in a man depends on his availability. But reality is more complicated than that. Single women often

complain that 'all the good men are taken' but the truth seems to be that being already taken makes a man more attractive. Single women are more attracted to a man if they think he is already attached, the 'logic' being that if he is without a partner there must be something wrong with him. No such 'mate poaching' preference is observed either for men, who pursue female targets fairly indiscriminately, or for women who are themselves attached (they prefer single targets).

Cultural similarities (and differences)

There is much consistency across cultures as to who is attractive. The principles of averageness, symmetry and exaggerated gender apply equally in non-Western cultures. Infants as young as 2–3 months share the same standards of beauty as adults, preferring to look at faces that adults find attractive; hence standards of beauty cannot just be cultural artefacts. Biological factors (evolved instincts) are clearly involved and these universal preferences derive from signals of mate quality (indications of youth, health, fitness and fertility).

Some variations across time and place do need accounting for. Generally, they relate to the social aspects of mate quality (signals of wealth and status):

- The value of a suntan has varied throughout history. Pale skin was sought in Elizabethan days because exposure to the sun implied peasant status. From the industrial revolution onwards, a suntan became valued because workers were confined to mines, factories and offices, while the rich could afford foreign holidays.

- Thinness is prized in Western society, though particularly by women. Female models appearing in women's magazines are thinner than those featuring in men's magazines. Fleshiness of the kind associated with Turkish belly dancers may be valued where food deprivation means that only the rich can get fat.

- In tribal societies, strong men are prized because they make good hunters and fighters, but in modern societies physical strength is less clear an indicator: a skinny rich nerd may be more sought after as a husband.

- Youth (in women) is prized in Western society; less so in tribal cultures that venerate elders, where pendulous breasts may be preferred over those that are pert.

An interesting historical variation in standards of beauty is that men's perception of sex appeal depends upon the nation's economic health. Apparently, men and women seek fun when things are going well and support/security when times are bad.

What is familiar is attractive

We tend to value traits that are typical within our own group – for example, hairiness in Scots, smoothness in Chinese, large breasts in Hollywood and protruding buttocks in black African women. This highlights another explanation as to why average faces are attractive. We are most comfortable with patterns we have come to expect, since these are easier to process in the brain. This 'exposure' principle has been demonstrated using abstract stimuli like patterns of dots, but it generalises to human beauty.

Familiarity is a learning mechanism that helps to explain **genetic similarity attraction** – a tendency to prefer those closely related to and resembling ourselves. It seems we form a blueprint for what will be sexually attractive in adulthood based partly on our experience of our opposite-sex parent in early childhood (an element of truth in the Freudian idea of the 'Oedipus complex').

Familiarity also helps us to understand idolisation and our obsession with celebrities, even those that are totally vacuous or well-known simply because their face is seen repeatedly in the media.

Summary so far

Beauty and sex appeal are not inherent in stimulus patterns that are 'out there' but rooted in our responses to them. They are based on signals of health, reproductive and parental fitness, as well as exposure and familiarity. Of course, we are seldom conscious of the mechanisms and survival value of our choices but simply go on 'instinct'. Hopefully, though, the principles outlined above will help you to understand your choice of who you thought 'sexy'.

What about gay people?

Most of the above discussion has assumed heterosexuality, whereas surveys suggest that around 4% of men and 2% of women are primarily attracted by members of their own sex. With respect to beauty, most of the same principles apply for gay people (averageness, symmetry, smooth complexion, familiarity, etc.). As regards sex appeal, gender signals are still the key, only it is *same-sex* features that are sought rather than opposite-sex ones. Not all preferences are reversed, though. Gay men are usually attracted to younger partners (just like straight men) and lesbians are more concerned about personality traits like loyalty and kindness than purely physical attributes (like straight women).

Party time

Parties provide an interesting venue for examining body language, not just because social and sexual relationships are uppermost, but because people are usually drinking. Alcohol liberates and magnifies body language just as it makes people more verbally outspoken. Inhibitions are lowered and, shorn of the polite veneer, people's true motives, their lusts, hatreds and ambitions, come to the fore.

We go to parties mainly to meet people and get to know better those we have already met. We may also be looking for new sex partners. How do we know that others are available and attracted to us? The first clue is in self-presentation. Do they look as though they have 'come as they were', as they might appear on any day or night of the week? If they have made an effort to dress nicely, washed and combed their hair and applied make-up that enhances their looks, we may suppose they want to make a good impression in general. Of course, this doesn't guarantee that we will be targeted as the beneficiary; to assess this, we have to look to other cues (detailed below).

If a person has contrived some special effect (what social scientists call 'impression management') then we should ask what effect they are seeking to achieve.

- Have they dressed expensively so as to suggest wealth? Is it some kind of uniform that would indicate occupation or status?

- Is it something a little threatening like a leather jacket and jeans that might suggest rebelliousness?

- Perhaps it is sexually provocative (e.g. a low-cut purple blouse and split black skirt)?

- Are their clothes bright and revealing (extravert and permissive) or sombre and tightly buttoned (conformity and respectability)?

 When people are free to choose what to wear they cannot help but make a statement regarding their personality and intentions.

Something similar applies to hairstyles (Chapter 2). Long hair tends to look young, feminine and sexy in women, artistic or rebellious in men, while short-cropped hair tends to look tough or unfussy in both sexes. Blonde hair on a woman has babyish associations (as noted earlier) but since, in adulthood, it is usually a lifestyle choice, it can sometimes be a flag of sexual awareness and interest. Make-up likewise comes in various styles, some of which are 'come hither' and others not sexual.

Body language gives away much about new arrivals at a party. Nervous fidgeting like checking cuff-links and ear-rings, and self-comforting gestures like licking the lips or rubbing the chin, suggest that people are not entirely comfortable. Their general mood may be assessed by the amount of energy they emit and the cheerfulness of their smile. Happy people have a spring in their step, hold their head high, smile broadly and talk in an animated way. Depressed people move slowly and reluctantly and talk in a slurred monotone, and their body tends to curl around a fulcrum of their own navel, thus closing themselves off from the world. Certain types of laughter and agitated speech can also result from nervousness rather than optimism but this is usually obvious to the observer. Smoking and drinking imply a hedonist mode.

Given the vital things there are to notice about people when we first meet them, it is not surprising that we often forget to register their names. It is as if we realise their name is arbitrary while the other cues provide valuable information about what kind of people they are. Nevertheless, people's names are very important to them so it is crucial to make an effort and find a trick for remembering them if we want to impress them later on.

Are they an item?

One of the useful things to know about a couple is how into each other they are. Their potential availability depends on how strong the bond is between them. Some couples arrive in tight formation, fondling each other possessively. This proclaims that they are not 'on the make' but belong to each other and intend to go home together. Others bounce in independently, pretending they are not with the individual whose entrance was delayed by putting coats in the bedroom, and scanning the room superficially to see who is there that might interest them. Social, and perhaps also sexual, availability is signalled by such behaviour.

 All of the other signs of bonding described in Chapter 4 can also be used to confirm whether a couple are inseparable. This includes paying exclusive attention to each other's conversation and not looking over their shoulder to see who else is available. There may also be genuine smiles, mutual gaze, gratuitous touching, mirroring gestures and orienting bodies towards each other so as to exclude outsiders. When such behaviours are observed in a couple, attempts to get between them will be fruitless.

Do they fancy us?

If we are talking to a person to whom we are attracted and who does not seem attached to anyone else, how do we judge whether they are attracted to us? Most obviously they will emit flirtation signals such as attentiveness, preening and hair tossing, tilting their head back and exposing vulnerable and private areas of the body like their neck, inner wrists and thighs. They may show any of the warm signals (covered in Chapter 4) such as smiling, extended eye contact, mirroring and orienting their body towards us. They will also show a greater willingness to discuss intimate and personal details about themselves and their lives.

KEY TERM

Preening refers to any attempt to make one-self more attractive and is seen in both men and women. It includes things like brushing the hair off the face, adjusting one's clothing, straightening the tie, looking in mirrors, pulling in the stomach and drawing oneself up to full height. Such gestures reflect a person's concern to appear at their best (youthful and vigorous) and suggest that they are in courtship mode directed at somebody close to hand (hopefully ourselves).

If the person is particularly 'into you', then indications of emotional arousal may be noted. These include heavier breathing, beating heart, tensing of muscles, and flushing of the cheeks or neck. They may betray themselves with flustered behaviour like shuffling the feet, twiddling fingers, stilted, stammering conversation and minor accident-proneness. When people are sexually attracted to us they also find socially acceptable ways of touching and making body contact.

When people are excited by what they see, the pupils of their eyes tend to expand. Centuries before scientists studied this effect, Chinese jade dealers and Arab traders haggling in the market place were known to use this cue to assess interest in their wares. Medieval Italian courtesans created the effect artificially using a drug called *belladonna* ('beautiful woman'). This was because they recognised that enlarged pupils are attractive to men. Interestingly, the effect is often unconscious in that people find large pupils attractive without being able to put their finger on the reason why they find one person more attractive than another.

A kiss is not just a kiss

The kiss is a special kind of touching that has many meanings. In some social situations it has no sexual connotation, for example, when greeting family or an old friend, wishing someone a happy birthday or saying goodbye at the end of a party. Still, the manner in which the kiss is delivered and received says much about the feelings of the two people involved.

The double-cheek kiss, as performed by politicians and fashionable people, which bounces from side to side with no risk of a wet landing in between, is perhaps the most cold and formal. A kiss to one side of the face can be made more intimate by being held longer. The lips may be 'worked' sensuously and it may be directed to erogenous zones like the neck and earlobe. A kiss direct on the lips is a higher level of intimacy still and the signal can be magnified in a variety of ways, such as staying with it for a long time or introducing the tongue into the mouth of the other.

We can tell much about how a kiss on the mouth is received. If an attempt to kiss a person full on the lips is deflected by the person turning their cheek and presenting their cheek instead, then a message is imparted ('Back off – you're getting too fresh', or perhaps 'Not now, my spouse is watching'). A miscalculated tongue in the mouth may even provoke a (well-deserved) slap in the face.

THINK ABOUT IT

Although kissing is an obvious expression of intimacy, its exact form varies from culture to culture. However, the most common mouth-to-mouth form of kissing is a way of demonstrating trust and closeness. It may function as a test of the health and immune system of the other person and to consolidate bonding through the exchange of pheromones emitted by the skin and saliva. Anthropologists have suggested that kissing derives from the mouth-to-mouth feeding of babies by mothers with pre-masticated food, a practice still observed in some African tribes. Women particularly enjoy kissing, perhaps because they have a superior sense of smell and are more fussy about with whom they exchange body fluids.

Tone of voice

If people compliment us on the way we look and say nice things to us, that is obviously a sign that they like us. However, not everybody has the confidence to do this openly. Many people are too shy or afraid that such an approach might seem forward. Therefore we may gain more information from a person's tone of voice.

Affection is indicated by soft, low resonant sounds and by a slightly slurred, purring delivery with regular rhythm and upward inflexion. Courting couples are described as 'whispering sweet nothings' to each other, which sums up such speech characteristics.

Sex differences in flirting

Men and women flirt in slightly differing ways, as we saw in Chapter 4. Men tend to pull their stomach in, tense their muscles so as to look taller and stronger, and confront their 'quarry' in an almost aggressive way. Their chest may be thrust forward like an ape's. They fix the woman with an intimate gaze and may draw attention to their genital area by spreading their legs wide apart and thrusting their thumbs inside their belt like a cowboy about to draw, their fingers triangulating on their crotch.

Women also stand face-to-face and make their private areas more accessible, but they have a more subtle range of gestures. These include diverting their eyes after being caught making contact, moistening their lips with their tongue, leaving their mouth slightly open in a manner symbolic of the genitals (pouting) and flicking their hair off their face. Flirting women may also echo the behaviour of the man they are talking to, or fondle 'phallic' objects such as wine glasses, salt cellars and cigarettes in a suggestive way.

Another classic female signal is to exaggerate the hip roll when walking. This 'Monroe wiggle' emphasises the large, child-bearing hips of a woman and signals fertility. Research reveals that when women are at mid-cycle (their most fertile phase) they take several seconds longer to walk a short distance because their bottom is wiggling more.

Beware the proteans

Men tend be over-optimistic in courtship, being prone to mistaking mere friendliness as flirtation.

Oxford anthropologists have found that men are often triggered into making a pass by women sending out subtle, deceptive flirtation signals called **proteans** (named after the Greek river god who constantly changed form to escape his enemies). Although often read by men as a 'go' signal, this is in fact an instinctive screening device, a form of subconscious interrogation used by women to assess whether a man is worth pursuing further. Women blitz men in the first minutes of meeting with erratic and ambiguous signals designed to manipulate them into showing their hand and, not surprisingly, these often lead to confusion in men.

According to Oxford researchers, flirting proper begins with the 'copulatory gaze', where intense eye contact is momentarily broken with lifting or lowering of the eyes. This is followed by smiles, body mirroring, coy looks and head-tossing. When a woman strokes her hair for a few seconds she is transmitting a subconscious signal that she is grooming herself for the man. The sequences have been likened to those seen in the courtship dances of birds and other animals. Interestingly, although it is widely believed that men take the initiative in flirting, around two-thirds of flirtatious encounters actually begin with some kind of subtle invitation from the woman.

Pseudo-flirting

Flirting is sometimes intended just to tease, rather than actually seduce. There may be complex underlying motives, such as proving one's irresistible charms to oneself or keeping a partner on their toes by making them jealous. It may also occur just out of politeness, to make the recipient feel good ('courtesy flirting') or simply to practise one's seductive skills.

Some people play 'hard to get', for example insulting a potential partner in order to get their attention. This strategy works on the theory that lowering a person's self-esteem pushes them down the social hierarchy and makes them more vulnerable to subsequent flattery. They become relieved and grateful that you seem to like them after all. However, this is a ploy that easily backfires in that the target may just move off decisively.

Clearly, there is a danger of being over-simplistic when interpreting people's body language in a party situation, as elsewhere. While, in the main, people who like us will smile, approach, seek eye contact, lean towards us, touch us and kiss passionately, we need to remember that they have egos and some have a particular fear of rejection. They may also wish to conceal their attraction because of the presence of a current spouse or partner. For various reasons, people may do the opposite of what would normally display their attraction. An interaction between strangers who are mutually attracted usually proceeds with some caution and depends upon perceived reciprocation at each stage. A misreading by one party could cause the spiral to be thrown into reverse, never to recover.

 When you are in a social situation like a party or a bar with some time to spare, try observing the women around you and see how many of the following devices you can tick off on the list. Many of these come from a list compiled by anthropologist Simon Sheppard, author of *The Tyranny of Ambiguity*. Many concern little signals emitted by a woman in the presence of a man they want to attract but who is slow on the uptake; others may be designed merely to tease (thus giving reassurance of her desirability). See how many of them you can observe – perhaps in competition with a friend.

1. Accidental touching – the woman nudges or brushes against the target man. She may even contrive a full body collision.

2. Looking forlorn – the woman suddenly looks terribly sad in the proximity of the target man.

3. Body pout – a part of the woman's body is protruded or displayed.

4. Empty glass – the gentle shake of an empty glass ('Buy me a drink').

5. Grimace – a response to attention, as though in extreme pain.

6. Preening – adjustment of clothes or hair in presence of target.

7. Looking helpless – deliberately evoking male caretaking instincts.

8. Head cant – leaning head to lower height and mimic baby leaning on mother.

9. Bottom wiggle – walking past the man with buttocks rolling in a display of fertility.

10. Challenge – a subtle display of defiance.

11. Foot stamp – the foot is stamped audibly on the floor.

12. Hesitation – uncertainty is displayed in an action or direction of movement.

13. Looking back – after passing the target, she turns and looks back over her shoulder.

14. Playful abandon – careless and playful gesture indicating receptivity.

15. Gaze diversion – being caught looking at target and rapidly looking away.

16. Hair flick – flexible hair is a self-conscious youth display.

17. Shoe dangle – dangling a shoe on the toes as symbolic of undressing.

18. Fondling objects – a glass or salt cellar is suggestively fondled.

19. Waving keys – target male is invited to follow.

20. Not saying goodbye – also sometimes a cue that the man should follow.

Tips for men: How to impress a woman

Being handsome is a good start in attracting a woman but the way a man plays his cards is also important. What has been said above can used as the basis of practical advice to a man about how he might succeed with a woman who particularly appeals to him. Some of the key principles of seduction, based on body language and general psychological principles, are as follows:

1. **Show that you are interested**: Make your intention explicit but not your language. Engage her in warm,

appreciative eye contact. Say 'I want you' through smiling eyes rather than with words.

2. **Compliment and provide for her**: Make compliments that are genuine, not transparent flattery or smarm. Show you are a good provider with personal gifts like flowers, perfume, jewellery, clothing and quality meals.

3. **Think about setting**: If you live in a nice place, arrange your meetings at your place rather than hers. If your dwelling is less than impressive, go for a romantic setting that is novel to her, be it a pub, restaurant, gallery, concert or holiday destination.

4. **Demonstrate competence**: If activities such as sailing or dancing are involved in your excursions, it is better if they are things you are competent in rather than those that are likely to show you in a failing light.

5. **Show ego-strength and security**: Don't talk about yourself excessively, especially not in a neurotic or boastful way. Don't try too hard to sell yourself – this suggests that you think you are really not good enough for her and she is bound to accept your evaluation.

6. **Organise distracting and relaxing stimuli**: Soft lights, classical music, natural settings of trees, flowers and beaches, warmth and alcohol are all conducive to a good date.

7. **Maintain self-discipline**: Convey your own confidence, always assuming a successful outcome. Avoid making any moves that are likely to be blocked or rejected by your date, which would not only be unpleasant for her but would also undermine your rapport and confidence.

8. **Tantalise**: Don't move too fast. Don't invade her space or touch her if she is unready or uninterested. Try to hold as much in reserve as possible. Find an erogenous zone that is not too obvious or threatening, e.g. the neck or earlobe, and only progress if and when she wants you to do so.

9. **Be sensitive**: A woman must be treated as an individual. Learn about her preferences and take note how she responds to your attentions. Be sincere and thoughtful rather than cunning and exploitative.

10. **Be clean and nicely presented**: Make sure you are washed, with deodorant and subtle cologne. Your clothes should be in good repair and appropriate for the occasion.

Tips for women: How to impress a man

A similar list of suggested behaviours can be offered to women who want to seduce a man they have their eye on but who might need a little extra encouragement.

1. **Appear clean**: Wash your hair and hands in particular and be bathed and sweet-smelling. Clean your teeth before a date. These things are also important for men, but go to the top of the list for women.

2. **Don't smoke**: This is the biggest single turn-off to a non-smoking man, especially if he is looking for a long-term partner. If you're not keen to kick the habit for a man though, you might as well be up-front about it.

3. **Don't get drunk**: Being out of control puts you at risk on a date, and it doesn't show you in your best light.

4. **Wear provocative clothing**: Let your clothes show your best attributes in an enticing, natural way that doesn't make you feel uncomfortable. Appear touchable – not trussed up, inaccessible or afraid of getting your hair mussed.

5. **Be flirtatious**: Do something a little cheeky, provoking him in some minor way that might arouse his desire to touch you, e.g. tousling his hair or running away with something that is his. If you are dancing with someone else, make a sexy display while throwing glances at him.

6. **Act coy and coquettish**: Be caught looking at him admiringly, perhaps over the shoulder of someone else you are talking to. Show sexual awareness by averting your gaze. Shyness, vulnerability and blushing are usually attractive to men.

7. **Use symbolic caresses**: Touch your own lapels or thighs dreamily. Open your lips and moisten them tenderly with your tongue. Play with objects like a salt-cellar or your wine glass in a suggestive way.

8. **Make him feel accomplished**: Ask him to instruct you in something he is good at, e.g. playing pool, tennis, swimming, astronomy. Sports that involve physical demonstrations are particularly advantageous. But don't let him have all the glory …

9. **Be amusing and light-hearted**: Try not to be heavy and serious all the time on first dates. People consistently rate a sense of humour high in the attributes they're looking for in a partner. Be playful and make him laugh.

Not everything on these lists will work for you and the person you're trying to attract. While human nature is basically unchanged, remember to take your cues from the other person and modify how you use these tips based on the individual, their preferences and behaviours.

9. Stress fractures

The modern world is fast-paced and involves a great deal of stress. Communications have advanced to the extent that we are effectively 'on call' 24/7, even when we are supposed to be on holiday. Mobile phones were once taboo in leisure situations, now many people use their phones in restaurants and parties, and even on a golf course. Many of us feel under pressure as a result of such 'advances' and it doesn't just apply to top executives. Having too much to do in too little time creates stress – but perhaps not so much as losing your job, an experience that is becoming increasingly common. We have never had more freedom as to where we live or how we arrange our social affairs than we do today, but these very choices are a potential source of stress in themselves. There are few things more stressful than moving house or changing a long-term partner.

We experience plenty of stress but how we respond to it depends on our personality. What's intolerable to one individual is seen as an exciting challenge by another. But there comes a point where almost anyone will feel overwhelmed and unable to cope. This is when the signs of stress will be seen by the outside observer.

All stressed out

How can we tell when someone is under stress? Stress is primarily indicated by activation of the body's natural alarm system, called the 'fight/flight reaction'. This has two components: (1) An immediate neurological reaction, sometimes called the 'startle response', which is apparent when someone jumps in fright or blinks to protect their eyes from damage when a sudden, unexpected stimulus occurs. (2) The slower acting effects of adrenaline, a hormone secreted into the bloodstream causing general physiological arousal. Among the effects of adrenaline are an increase in heart rate and blood pressure, heavier breathing, facial flushing and sweating of the palms. These are paralleled by changes in the distribution of energy supplies around the body in preparation for emergency action, which might take the form of either running (fear) or fighting (aggression).

Some of the telltale signs of stress are these:

1. Physiological signs of fear/anxiety, e.g. the pulse becomes rapid, sometimes to the extent of being visible, there is sweating on the brow, audible breathing, an increase in blink rate and alterations in colour of the complexion between pallid and flushed (due to the blood being redirected to muscles and brain).

2. Saliva is inhibited so the mouth is dry, causing a speaker to drink more frequently.

3. Eyebrows are raised so that the eyes appear wide open and there are wrinkles on the brow.

4. The lips are stretched so that the mouth forms a rectangular or oblong pattern.

5. An increase in facial movements of all kinds, such as frowning and various little twitches and grimaces, some of them very fleeting.

6. Hands are clasped firmly together, causing the knuckles to go white. At the same time the thumbs may be worked in an agitated way.

7. The stressed individual may be observed to pace about randomly. (This is due to a need to burn off the excess adrenalin that is being generated by worry and preparing the body for some kind of action. If no effective, directed action is possible, then random activity occurs instead.)

8. If stuck in their chair, the stressed person shows an increase in the number of postural shifts, rocking and squirming movements, as though they would really like to escape the situation.

9. Scratching the head, finger tapping, fiddling with one's watch or buttons are other displacement ('fill-in') activities seen in people who are physically or psychologically uncomfortable but unable to escape the situation.

10. Movements with special significance include the collar pull ('I'm getting hot under the collar'), the ear rub ('I've

heard enough'), the eye rub ('I've seen enough') and the neck scratch ('I'm not sure I agree').

11. Self-comforting gestures, like touching and embracing oneself, occur more often. The stressed individual may suck a finger, put a finger or pencil in the mouth, or bite their nails. Whether or not one accepts the psychoanalytic argument that these oral behaviours represent nipple substitution, they certainly denote regression and hence insecurity.

12. Smokers have an increased desire to strike up a cigarette (another nipple substitute?).

13. An increase in defensive ('barrier') signals is observed, e.g. folding the arms in front of the body so as to set up a shield.

14. Adjusting cuff-links or jewellery provides an excuse for having one's hands out in front of the body, thus providing another form of defence equivalent to a boxer's guard. This is seen particularly in politicians and diplomats who are off their home territory.

15. Vulnerable parts of the body, like wrists, neck and thighs are tucked away so as to be less visible and accessible (e.g. clasping the hands across the genitals or crossing the legs).

16. A closed stance and a tendency to curl up into a ball like a hedgehog is indicative of insecurity.

17. People under stress tend to stand further away from others, almost as though they want to stay out of range of being hit.

18. Speech errors, hesitations, minor stammers and voice tremors occur with greater frequency under stress (as in *The King's Speech*). Some people talk more quickly when stressed so that they sound flustered and are more likely to 'trip over their tongue'.

19. There is a decrease in eye contact. The eyes may even be kept closed for brief periods as if to provide intermittent relief from unpleasant, threatening stimuli.

20. Submissive and false smiles (as opposed to enjoyment smiles) tend to increase in frequency. As already noted, false smiles are most obviously detected because they appear at the mouth only, not around the eyes. The submissive smile is effectively saying 'I am harmless, don't hit me'. The smile may also be used as an attempt to conceal anxiety, helping one to appear more confident than one is feeling inside.

21. At times yawning seems to stem from stress because of its link with tiredness, but it might equally mean that the person is bored. Since yawns are contagious they may also denote empathy; reciprocal yawning occurs most often among family and friends who are comfortable in each other's company. These distinctions make

yawning an ambiguous signal and a full assessment of the background circumstances is needed.

22. When stress becomes extreme, a kind of compulsive restraint may occur. This represents a recognition by the individual that they are close to 'overload' and need to reduce input.

23. In the business context, the person under stress may be seen to organise their notes and pencils on the desk in front of them, the physical equivalent of tidying their mind.

Apart from these things, most of which can be instantly observed, a stressed person will show various longer-term symptoms like sleeplessness, loss of appetite, digestive problems, breathlessness, dizzy spells, perhaps even panic attacks. These are slowly developing problems that are best observed by those they live with.

Causes of stress

While most of the body language signals described above are indicative of anxiety of some sort, they do not necessarily tell us what is causing that stress. Often it is because the individual's life situation is problematic or uncomfortable for some reason. Perhaps they are ill-prepared for an impending examination, are in fear of losing their job, or their domestic arrangements are unravelling. There are a great many reasons why one might be under stress.

However, we sometimes attribute stress to immediate surroundings when in fact it goes deeper and is unrelated to what is happening in the life of the person. Some forms of anxiety and depression seem to emanate from within, and these are particularly likely to need professional help.

 It should also be made clear that not all stress is necessarily bad. Short-term stress responses are a healthy way of reacting to threatening situations. In fact, a history of exposure to mild and intermittent stress helps to build coping mechanisms that provide immunity to later trauma. It is only long-term, or 'chronic' stress that is ultimately damaging to health.

Stress and anger

Most of the stress indicators described above are indicators of fear or anxiety. However, adrenaline can prompt fight as well as flight, so stress may sometimes emerge as irritability or anger. The signs of anger are as follows:

1. A deep frown, with eyebrows pulled low on the brow so the eyes are half-closed.

2. Clenching of the fist, as though ready to punch.

3. General tightening of muscles throughout the body.

4. A compressed mouth, with the lower jaw and teeth protruding.

5. Because the jaw is clenched the angry person may grind their teeth or talk out of the side of their mouth.

6. A flushed face.

7. Breathing heavily through the nose like a snorting bull.

8. Head thrust forward as if to butt the foe.

9. Higher pitch and increased volume in the voice. Other indications of anger include a threatening whisper or sudden, intermittent loud words. Yelling denotes extreme rage.

The display of anger represents a preparation for fighting or a threat to attack. Most of the connections are obvious. The tightly compressed mouth protects the jaw and teeth, the frown protects the eyes, while the red face is due to faster circulation of the blood around the body. Anger and fear are both products of the sympathetic nervous system and they often appear mixed to some degree, as though the individual is keeping their options open as to whether they should fight or flee the situation.

Crying and weeping

The sound of crying is used mainly by infants as a distress signal. This is the basic means by which they gain the attention and hence the help of their parents. Many animals also cry, producing a whimpering kind of sound that evokes caretaker instincts in humans as well as their own species.

Adult humans seldom cry audibly, except when they are suffering acutely. Occasionally, when badly hurt or frightened, they will produce the kind of scream that is the stuff of horror movies to alert others and solicit help.

THINK ABOUT IT

Adults weep tears when emotionally distressed more often than they cry audibly. This is a basic response to pain and extreme unhappiness, even though its original function was to clear grit away from the eyes. This is a striking illustration of the fact that emotional hurt has much in common with physical pain. The neurology and physiology involved is similar.

Tears are produced by lachrymal glands behind the upper eye. They wash over the eye and would normally be drained out through the nose via the corner of the eye. However, if the face is contorted by emotional pain this drainage system is blocked and the tears roll down over the face. This is a powerful emotional signal in humans and will evoke sympathy even more powerfully when performed silently. Adding sound to weeping can actually reduce the amount of sympathy felt by others. People are more likely to be impressed by the 'brave face' that goes with silent tears because it is clear that the crying is truly heartfelt and not a just a cynical attempt to solicit help.

Spotting stress in yourself
How many of the following signs do you notice in yourself?

1. You put things off that really should be done today.

2. You grumble and moan a lot.

3. You sometimes feel little twitches in your face.

4. You are inclined to snap at people who are only trying to help.

5. You flare up and lose your temper over nothing.

6. You frequently suffer from constipation.

7. You feel anxious a great deal of the time.

8. You talk a great deal about your worries without doing anything constructive to solve them.

If you recognise more than two or three of these early stress signs in yourself, then the time may have come to take stock of your lifestyle. Failure to address these early indicators of stress may leave you prone to more serious physical symptoms such as strokes or a heart attack.

The good life
Stress amounts to a form of overload, so in order to relax and prosper you may need to review your timetable and

commitments to see if adjustments can be made to reduce the demands on your resources. A healthy lifestyle is also an important way of combating stress.

1. Don't let your telephone or email dominate your day; if necessary switch them off and deal with them only during a set time slot.

2. Avoid wasting precious time on social networking sites such as Facebook or Twitter.

3. If you have several things to do in a day, take them one at a time and complete each task before moving on to the next one. This provides a series of small goals and achievements that makes your workload more manageable.

4. Prioritise your commitments and limit your working hours to allow time for exercise and leisure. Outdoor activities such as walking, swimming or golf are most beneficial because, apart from the actual exercise, they provide fresh air, changing scenery and exposure to sunlight (which restores stocks of vitamin D).

5. Get a proper amount of sleep – around 7–8 hours every night. Sleep is promoted by avoiding caffeine and alcohol at bedtime and waking up at approximately the same time each morning. Sleeping pills are best avoided because they do not give natural, restful sleep and can be habit-forming.

6. Eat well, avoiding too many snacks and sweets. Drink plenty of water, avoiding fizzy, sugary drinks and espresso coffee whenever possible.

7. It may help to learn some techniques of relaxation like yoga, meditation, slow breathing or positive imagery. There are plenty of self-help books and evening classes along these lines.

8. If all such things do not help you cope, it may be time to seek medical help. Your GP or local health centre is a good place to start.

Tips on taking control

If you feel stress mounting in your work or personal relationships it may be useful to have an armoury of stress-busting tricks that will prevent you from lapsing towards panic.

1. Take some slow, deep breaths, making the exhalation (breathing out) phase a little longer each time.

2. Say 'relax' to yourself silently as you exhale.

3. Concentrate on reducing tension in your muscles, focusing on one area at a time. This technique, called 'progressive relaxation', usually recommends starting from the feet. Consciously tighten and then relax them a few times, then move on, perhaps to the legs, and so on throughout the rest of the body.

4. If you simply can't relax, at least try to maintain your composure. Stay as still and poised as possible and avoid fiddling with your belongings, clothes or hair.

5. If your raised adrenaline makes you impossibly restless, then find an excuse to do something physical – perhaps collecting empty plates, or mowing the lawn. This will burn up the spare energy and look less conspicuous than pacing up and down.

6. You may notice that you are sweating and that your heart is racing. Tell yourself that this is because you are 'excited', not 'anxious' or 'stressed'. In this way you can 'befriend' your bodily agitation and look to its benefits.

7. Try to keep looking at the person you are dealing with. Looking away or down at the floor comes across as shifty and you may increase any antagonism they feel towards you.

8. Don't try to appease the other person by forcing a smile; if it is not heartfelt it will be easily identified as false and this may be worse than no smile at all. If, however, you can find a pretext for a genuine smile, then go for it – it is bound to improve diplomatic relations.

 Think back over your life to an incident in which you really 'put your foot in it' and suffered intense embarrassment as a result.

Most of us can recall some episode from our past in which we wished the ground would open up and swallow us. Now ask yourself what exactly were you feeling and why? Do you think the other people around noticed your embarrassment? Did you dig yourself into a deeper hole by attempting an explanation? The chances are that you did, and this is one of the reasons the incident is burned in your brain.

Embarrassment is a very specific and often very powerful form of stress. The first thing to note is that almost certainly it involves other people, since embarrassment is a very *social* emotion. It usually implies that we have unintentionally breached some rule of etiquette that has diminished us in the eyes of those around us. We feel bad because a gap has opened up between the way we wanted to be perceived and the way we have actually come across.

Interestingly, the fact that we *show* our embarrassment might be our redemption. Unless we are seen to cringe and blush and make awkward attempts to explain and apologise, we compound the social transgression by not even registering that we have committed a gaffe. We may make reparation by allowing others to laugh at our stupidity, thus allowing them to wallow in their sense of superiority, though of course they would justify their laughter as 'making light of the incident'. 'Cringe comedy' is central to the work of certain comedians, notably Ricky Gervais (in *Extras*) and Larry David (in *Curb Your Enthusiasm*), who dig themselves progressively into embarrassing situations.

Stressed relationships

Is it possible to tell if a couple are troubled in their relationship? Superficially, it might seem that they are getting on very well, but there are some giveaways that might tell a different story. Oxford psychologist Peter Collett has listed a number of indicators that suggest a relationship could be headed for the rocks:

1. If kissing is not synchronised (the same on both sides) it implies that one member of the pair is uncomfortable performing that gesture.

2. When a couple are facing each other, note which way their feet are pointing. If one has their feet pointing away from their partner it suggests they would rather be somewhere else.

3. Lack of eye contact or a chin tucked into the chest are signs that intimacy is lacking.

4. When a person is lying about a relationship, their blink rate triples from around 20 times a minute to about 60 times per minute.

5. If a couple hold hands without pressing their palms together it suggests they are drifting apart.

6. When a woman flicks her hair and looks away while she is with her partner it suggests she is trying to get the attention of somebody else.

Charles and Diana

One of the most famous instances of a doomed relationship is that of Prince Charles and Diana, Princess of Wales. When their relationship was announced they looked awkward together from the outset. Their arms were not linked and they were not in step when they walked. Charles hardly looked at her during the interviews and spent much time fiddling with his cuffs. Asked if they were in love, he famously said 'Yes, whatever that means'. Again, at their wedding Charles barely glanced at Diana, looking mostly at the ground, the ceiling, anywhere else rather than at her. He was also seen to rub his cheek, which could symbolise the wiping away of a tear. Subsequent developments suggest he may have been thinking about his soul-mate Camilla through much of the ceremony. No such problems were observed with the union of William and Kate.

---

10. Faking sincerity

The late American comedian George Burns once said that 'an actor's chief virtue is sincerity – if he can fake that he's made'. Acting, as well as many other performance arts such as speech-making, may indeed be considered the art of faking sincerity.

It is said that 'all the world's a stage', but it is equally true that the stage represents the whole of the real world. Actors and performers draw on the principles of body language in plying their trade and can therefore profit from a study of its principles in producing an effective performance.

In portraying emotion, all the various aspects of posture, gesture and facial expression described in this book can be employed. For example, fear or shock can be displayed in the following ways:

1. Freezing of movement and silence (avoidance of detection and locating source of danger).

2. Eyes wide open and alert, with head moving from side to side (also for purpose of locating the threat).

3. Body muscles sprung (ready for hasty escape once optimal direction is determined).

4. Breathing pronounced (so as to increase oxygen supply to muscles).

5. Mouth stretched wide horizontally (approximation to submission smile).

6. The seeking of physical contact or proximity to other people or objects. If walls or trees are available, the frightened individual will gravitate towards them, hold on to them or flatten themselves against them in order to feel less exposed/more secure.

As we have seen, worry or anxiety is indicated by nervous movements such as pacing up and down, scratching the head, snapping the fingers and punching the palm. This may be understood as a problem-solving mode, maintaining arousal and 'tuning up' the brain by providing a continually changing perspective on the environment that might prompt a new idea. Restless movement may also represent behavioural conflict (not being quite sure what to do next) or it may be due simply to the need to burn up excess adrenaline. There are also ways of suggesting anxiety through facial expression (see Chapters 3 and 9).

Relaxation is the opposite of fear and anxiety and is conveyed primarily by a lack of muscle tension (i.e. not preparing for any emergency action). It is also indicated by the open teeth smile which, in contrast to percussive laughter, is a friendly, happy, appeasing kind of gesture.

It is easier for a performer who is suffering some degree of stage fright to portray fear, worry or anxiety than relaxation, because their performance anxiety can support or amplify the anxiety of the character in the play.

Moods are contagious

'Smile and the world smiles with you', it is said. This is true, but it is not true that we 'cry alone'. In portraying various emotions on stage, actors are assisted by the fact that emotions are contagious. When other people laugh, or feel sad, shocked or angry there is a fairly direct knock-on effect to other people. Emotions are thus readily passed from one person to another without a word being spoken. The survival value of mood contagion is obvious – animals reverberate to the moods of their own species because the presence of predators may need to be signalled without making a noise that would give away their whereabouts.

This is the origin of what we call empathy, the highly developed capacity of humans to know what others are feeling and to feel an echo of it in ourselves. It is made possible by what are called 'mirror neurons' in the brain that respond to what others are feeling by imitating it in ourselves. In the theatre, empathy enables us to identify with the characters and understand their plight at a direct, intuitive level. There is evidence that women are, on average, better equipped than men in using powers of observation and empathy to understand the emotions of others. Research has shown that women consistently outperform men when it comes to processing facial expressions of emotion and indeed body language signals of all kinds.

 Do women make better actors than men?
A team of Cambridge psychologists set about making a video for training autistic people in identifying various emotions. Actors and actresses were asked to create an expression from a cue word like 'hysterical' or 'brazen'. To check that they had succeeded, a panel of volunteers were asked to match the expression with the word. The women actors did better in creating a face that could be correctly identified. You can repeat this experiment at home by agreeing a list of words that describe emotions and having people try to simulate them on video. The betting is that women's expressions will be guessed by others more consistently than those of men and that women will identify the emotions of others more accurately. This is what is sometimes known as women's intuition.

As we saw in Chapter 3, when men and women are asked to imagine emotional situations, women show more muscle activity in their face. They also report a more vivid experience of the emotion, so women may express more emotion because they *feel* more emotion.

Sinister expressions

You'll also remember from Chapter 3 that the left side of the face is generally more expressive than the right. When people are asked to create expressions of emotion and photos are taken of their face, the left and right sides of their face show appreciably different expressions. If the photos are divided down the middle and two complete faces reconstructed by mirroring, the picture made out of the left side of the face is more emotional than that derived from the right. Research shows that people are better able to identify the expression of the left face. This may come about because the right side of the brain, which has control of the left facial muscles, is superior at pattern processing. The practical implication of this for stage performance is that, other things being equal, the actor on stage left is better positioned to impress an audience than the actor on stage right.

Imaginative vs. technical approaches

There are two major schools of thought as to how a convincing portrayal is best achieved.

One approach is *technique*, meaning the deliberate manipulation of posture, gesture and tone of voice to signal appropriate feelings to an audience. The other is the *imaginative* approach, often referred to as '**the method**'. This means getting into the part in such a way that the actor feels the emotions that would be felt by the character in their situation within the drama.

Performance on the stage (and especially operatic acting) makes more use of whole-body postures that can communicate emotions at a distance compared with movie and TV acting, which is a much more intimate medium. Some great stage actors have difficulty in reducing their large-scale performance to the close-up world of the camera.

Method acting was greatly boosted by the advent of screen performances that required much more subtlety of expression than the big stage, which especially in the gaslight days needed flamboyant gestures. Some of the best-known movie actors, such as Marlon Brando, Dustin Hoffman and Marilyn Monroe, were associated with 'the method' as advocated by the famous Actors' Studio established in New York by acting teacher Lee Strasberg.

Emotional memory

'Method' actors like to make use of their 'emotional memory', recalling situations from their own past that are parallel to those of the character they are portraying and remembering how they felt at the time. For example, if they need to cry they may think of a moment of bereavement in their own life, perhaps the moment a favourite pet died. The presumption is that if the actor can truly conjure the feelings that would be felt by the character, then all the appropriate body movements and voice intonations will fall into place quite naturally and they will deliver a performance that comes across as sincere to the audience.

Say 'cheese'

Have someone film you creating two smiles. In the first smile, simply contrive it as though a photographer has asked you to say 'cheese'. For the second smile, try to recall some instance in your life that made you joyful and smile with that thought in mind. Now compare the two smiles. The fake smile probably just displays the teeth with the lips pulled back to reveal an artificially open (oblong) mouth. This artificial smile is often called 'cheesy' for obvious reasons. You may notice that it's not even on the two sides of the face. The warmly-felt smile (named a 'Duchenne smile' after the man who identified it) should involve the whole of the face, especially producing little wrinkles at the outer corners of the eyes and underneath. It's also likely to be more symmetrical from left to right. If no one is available to film you, the same comparison might be made just by studying yourself in a mirror and creating smiles by these two different methods.

Interestingly, American researchers have found that genuine smiles in photos of baseball players were predictive of how long they lived. Using group photos from the 1952 *Baseball Register*, they found that those showing genuine

(Duchenne) smiles were half as likely to die in any given year as non-smilers. Clearly positive emotions, as displayed in a smile, are good for the health.

There is no doubt some value in the imaginative approach to acting. We have already noted that skilled liars talk themselves into pretty much believing the deceit they are perpetrating in order to be more persuasive. This is what might be called 'method lying'. If they can succeed in what amounts to a kind of self-hypnosis they may even be able to pass a lie-detector test.

Possession syndrome

Some actors take 'the method' to extremes and lose control of the boundaries between fantasy and reality, confusing the role they are playing with their real lives. The two merge to the extent that they have trouble untangling them.

- Daniel Day-Lewis once fled the stage in a performance of *Hamlet* because he saw the ghost of his own father (the poet C. Day-Lewis).

- One Brazilian TV soap actor actually killed his on-screen girlfriend because her character was unfaithful in the scripted show.

- Undercover detectives who have to infiltrate drug gangs or terrorist organisations have been known to collaborate with the criminals or to experience intense 're-entry strain' when attempting to revert to their previous lives. Because a convincing portrayal is often a matter of life and death, they identify with the role they have assumed to the extent that they are unable to return comfortably to their real self.

The technical approach

Proponents of technical acting point out that imagination in itself is seldom sufficient in performing. Consciousness has to be divided to some extent, if only to allow control of practical things like where they are standing and which way they are facing and whether their voice can be clearly heard. Technical actors make the criticism that 'method' exponents are often so self-absorbed that they become inaudible (Marlon Brando and Sylvester Stallone being especially prone to mumbling).

 Critics point out that excessive displays of emotion may actually interfere with audience empathy. If an actor is too demonstrative the audience may 'stop travelling'. Rather than festering with internal emotions, the job of the actor is sometimes more equivalent to providing a 'blank canvas' on which the audience can project their own feelings.

When Noël Coward was directing *Nude With a Violin* he was approached by an earnest young actor asking for an in-depth analysis of the character he was playing. 'My dear boy,' Coward replied, 'never mind the motivation, just say the lines and don't trip over the furniture.' Of course, excessive technique can also be intrusive. Some critics say that in watching Laurence Olivier's Shakespearean performances (e.g. his film of *Othello*) they find themselves becoming more aware of a great actor going through his paces than the plight of the character.

The debate between technical and method actors is perennial. Technical performers think there are many things more important than summoning realistic emotions and that, anyway, an emotion can be generated by the appropriate gestures and postures. They maintain that it does not matter whether the performer feels the emotion; all that matters is that it is communicated to the audience. Method actors say this approach is limited and that modern audiences are so tuned in to the subtleties of performance that they will not be fooled by 'manufactured' feelings.

There is no doubt some truth in both arguments. Both imagination and technique are necessary for optimum performance and it may come down to a question of which is deficient and needs to be developed with a particular performer.

The gap between imagination and technique may not be as great as it first appears. Research by Paul Ekman, one of the leaders in the field, has established that if we flex our facial muscles into the patterns characteristic of joy, anger, sadness (or whatever), there are immediate effects in the nervous system that normally accompany these emotions. Expressions of happiness, for example, produced a lowered heart rate, while sadness led to lowered skin temperature and increased electrical conductance. In other words, it seems to be impossible to contrive the body language of emotions without feeling the emotion yourself to some extent. Ekman also found that people tend to mimic the emotional expressions of those around them, with the result that similar effects are induced in their own nervous system, consistent with the empathy phenomenon.

Use of feedback and modelling

Technical actors make use of a number of tricks in preparing for a role. One is to seek 'feedback', which can be achieved with the help of anything from mirrors and videos to having a close friend or partner supply candid criticism. This enables the performer to 'see themselves as others see them'. It is characteristic of technical actors that their focus of attention is 'out there' in the auditorium looking back, rather than inhabiting the character from the inside. The danger they face from feedback is that of damaged self-esteem. Friends and family need to be aware that their comments can have a negative impact on the performer's all-important self-confidence. Professional critics may have to be ignored because their comment is often so brutally honest as to be humiliating and ego-destructive.

Another 'technique' approach is that of 'modelling'. Observations of the accents and body language of suitable models are deployed in order to construct a character.

When Anthony Sher came to play Richard III he modelled the character on certain serial killers and predatory insects, all of which is detailed in his book *The Year of the King*. Peter Sellers' classic portrayal of Dr Strangelove included a somewhat comical German accent that he borrowed from an on-set technician and observations of a neurological condition called 'the alien hand', in which the patient experiences one of their hands as having a will of its own (in this case throwing up Nazi salutes that have to be pulled back down with the other hand).

Picturing perfection

Some performers (and sportspeople) model themselves on highly successful proponents of their skill. The amateur tenor, for example, may think of himself as Luciano Pavarotti as he steps out onto the stage, or the mediocre golfer may imagine that he is Tiger Woods as he drives off the tee. This enables them to model their performance on perfection as depicted in 'the mind's eye' and is a useful combination of technique and imagination.

TRY IT NOW!

Next time you have to deliver a performance, either artistic or sporting, try imagining you are the individual who is at the top of their game and see if this helps you give of your best.

Personality theory

A knowledge of personality theory (knowing how various personality traits link together) may help an actor in their trade. A tendency to be sociable and party-loving, for example, is more often associated with impulsiveness and irresponsibility than it is with control and conscientiousness. Recognition of such coherence can help produce a rounded, credible character.

Psychoanalytic theory may also be called upon to create a convincing character. For example, repressed sexuality may be represented by an actor who walks with minimal movement of the pelvis and tightly clenched buttocks ('uptight'). The man with a stiff military bearing may be seen as defending against anxiety, in particular the fear of losing control of his own behaviour. A woman who is very aloof and affected may be caught in conflict between flirtation and shyness.

THINK ABOUT IT

A famous application of Freudian theory to the stage was a production of *Hamlet*, starring Laurence Olivier, in which the Prince was clearly in the throes of an Oedipus complex, wanting to kill his step-father because he was sexually attracted to his mother (who was played by a younger than usual actress and whom he groped gratuitously in her bedroom). Around the same time, a production of *Othello* introduced the idea that Iago was motivated by lust for his master that was underlying his desire to destroy Desdemona. Such interpretations usually come from the director rather than the cast, and do not necessarily enhance the drama. However, it is useful for actors to know about and be open to such possibilities.

Body language of dance

The principles of posture and gesture apply very obviously to dance, whether classical or modern. Indeed, dance may be understood as the artistic extension of postural self-expression, with body movement used to amplify the connection between music and emotion.

There are two big dimensions in the body language of dance.

1. Central to the choreography pioneered by American Martha Graham, among others, is **contraction and expansion**, and particularly the progression from one into the other. When the body is curled up into a ball, with limbs contracted, a feeling of misery, submission and oppression is conveyed. As confidence and joy

are developed, gestures become more open and body space is increased. Finally, territory is expanded triumphantly and movement around the stage becomes faster and freer. In this way, the growth of dominance, self-esteem and freedom is depicted. Elements of this basic scenario are seen in many dance routines.

2. The second feature of the body language of dance concerns **exaggerations of gender signals**, particularly in partnered Latin dances or ballet. Male dancers tend to use abrupt, athletic movements with straighter body orientation and upward, expansive gestures of the limbs (arms and legs outstretched). They also cover a wider territory. Women are more graceful and rounded in their movements, with beauty and suppleness emphasised rather than strength and vigour.

REMEMBER THIS!!! Since many dance sequences are thinly disguised courtship rituals it is not surprising that the female partner tends to 'display' more often, while the male initiates more body contact and joint manoeuvres. Anthropologists note that the dancing of women in most cultures involves a kind of tease, with sexually suggestive gyrations and brief flashes of erotic stimuli (e.g. the whirling skirts of the French can-can, or the exposed flesh of a middle-Eastern 'belly dance') interspersed with 'escape' movements.

It may seem strange to describe male dancing as hyper-masculine when dancing in general is often regarded as an effeminate pursuit for men. Although androgynous as a person (e.g. having plastic surgery which gave him both masculine and feminine facial features) Michael Jackson's dance routines were macho in many respects (with vigour and athleticism, stiffly spread and defiantly planted legs, pelvic thrusting and blatant crotch-grabbing, raised fists and scowling). Understanding that gender signals are amplified in dance may help to focus a performance and make it more impressive.

What is charisma?

Charisma literally means 'charm' or 'magic' and it refers to the power of presence that some people seem to have quite naturally more than others. To some extent it can derive from institutional status. Being the headmaster, the boss of a large company or a member of the royal family carries a great deal of presumptive power. Henry Kissinger or Prince Charles are not especially prepossessing individuals but they came pre-equipped with socially bestowed power. However, charisma can certainly be boosted by attributes such as great beauty (Marilyn Monroe), strength (Arnold Schwarzenegger) or an exceptional singing voice (Tom Jones). Being unique (Yul Brynner) or just zany (Johnny Depp) can also contribute to charisma, as can simple familiarity (we previously mentioned vacuous celebrities). Then again, much of charisma is down to body language and the way we present ourselves, things that are more open to our own control (see Chapter 7).

Charismatic people do not have to be likeable. Some people who are cold, surly and abrasive can still be charismatic. Margaret Thatcher and Humphrey Bogart were not especially liked but few would deny they had the power of presence. Even out-and-out psychopaths like Saddam Hussein and the 'campus killer' Ted Bundy were impressive and charming. What seems to be central to charisma is self-assurance, defined by one anthropologist as 'the strength to resist the need to be liked'. In other words, charismatic people have a certain arrogance that conveys the message: 'I don't care whether you like me or not, I am here, not going away and doing exactly what I want to do.' It is this anti-social 'don't mess with me' aura that sometimes makes psychopaths attractive.

IF YOU REMEMBER ONE THING Of course, it's one thing to identify self-assurance as the key to charisma and another thing to contrive it. As noted in Chapter 7, social power is to some extent granted by others so it's easier to be self-assured when there is a history of others accepting our leadership. Nevertheless, the spiral can be altered at any point, so if we start to 'act' as though we are in control (however insecure we feel inside), the greater the chances are that others will concede power to us, thus raising our charisma.

Tips on giving a public speech

At some point in our life we are likely to be called upon to deliver a speech. We will thus end this chapter by providing some guidance as to how one can be an effective, persuasive speaker.

1. Prepare your material thoroughly, with more facts at your fingertips than you think you will actually need.

2. Know how you are going to start (often with some jocular or topical thought) and how you are going to end (usually reiterating your central message).

3. Don't dress down. It is important to feel comfortable in what you are wearing but better to make the mistake of looking too formal rather than too casual.

4. Let your stage fright work for you. You are bound to feel some symptoms of anxiety, stress or agitation (everybody does), but these will be less apparent to your audience than they are to you. As noted above, you can befriend your anxiety by thinking of it as 'excitement' rather than 'nervousness'. It is worth remembering that most people give their finest performance when they are a bit emotionally aroused (to an extent that feels uncomfortable to themselves). This lends electricity to the delivery.

5. Don't be disconcerted by odd members of the audience who appear bored or distracted. They probably

have their own agenda and it has little to do with how well you are performing. Focus your attention on those who seem to be in tune with you and returning positive signals.

6. Expect that one or two things will probably go wrong somewhere along the line. Rather than panic and try to cover them up, you will come across as more likeable if you publicly recognise the glitch and make light of it. (The comedian Tommy Cooper made an entire career out of this principle after setting out to be a magician and some of his tricks went wrong.)

7. However badly you think your talk has gone, appear proud of it at the end. Your closing statement is what will be taken away from the talk most saliently – and the chances are you are wrong about how badly you were being received in any case.

Appendix 1: The image makers

In the modern world there are many spin doctors and consultants who advise people on how to present themselves in dress and how to impress with their body language. They may be used either for general 'life coaching' or for specific purposes, like preparing a politician for a TV debate or an accused person who wants to appeal to the judge and jury in their trial.

Richard Nixon is widely supposed to have lost the presidential election to Kennedy because, in the first-ever TV debate between the candidates, he looked tired, sickly and shadowy around the chin. Former British prime minister Lady Thatcher was advised to wear true-blue suits with soft bows at the neck and to lower her voice tone to appear less strident. To what extent this contributed to her success is not known, but by contrast one of her opponents who eschewed any such makeover, Michael Foot, was nicknamed 'Worzel' (a fictional scarecrow) by the media and crashed to the biggest-ever election defeat.

High-profile trials, especially in the US, now employ consultants who advise on jury selection, wardrobe and body language. Among the cases in which the outcome may have been tilted by image gurus was that of O.J. Simpson, who was advised to wear demure, well-cut, but not ostentatious suits. His defence counsel, Robert Shapiro, would occasionally place an affectionate hand on his shoulder to make him appear likeable. Simpson's acting skills (he had been in several films) may also have helped to persuade the jury of his innocence, against a tide of circumstantial evidence.

The Menendez brothers, accused of shooting their parents to speed up their inheritance, were presented with carefully combed hair and similar pastel jerseys, in order to make them look young and vulnerable and thus reinforce their defence that they had been physically and sexually abused by their parents. At one point, their female attorney leaned across to one of brothers and picked lint off his clothes, like a doting mother. Again, they managed to split a jury against overwhelming evidence.

It is difficult to assess just how influential the image makers are in today's world but the importance of first impressions combined with the rising influence of visual media suggests that the money invested in them could pay rich dividends.

Appendix 2:
How to be a good boss/
How to deal with a bad boss

How to be a good boss

The following are some tips on how to be an effective and respected boss. Some of them relate to body language but most amount to common decency and consideration:

1. Motivate by positive rewards and incentives, not fear of punishment.

2. Praise your employees in public and criticise them only in private.

3. Give credit where credit is due; never claim credit for the achievements of others.

4. Gain the respect of employees by taking a personal interest in them and their problems.

5. Once you have delegated a task to an employee allow them to do it in their own way.

6. Make it clear that 'your door is always open' if they have a problem to discuss.

7. Be a good listener. Let them know what your expectations are but be open to feedback concerning their thoughts on how success in a project may be achieved.

8. As far as possible, let them settle disputes with other staff themselves without intervening in favour of one or the other.

9. Be tolerant and understanding of personal problems that may arise and allow some leeway as regards time off when a life crisis has occurred.

10. Keep it light. Try to maintain a sense of fun in the workplace so that your staff are happy to come to work.

How to deal with a bad boss

1. Try to agree with them as much as possible without compromising your own values and efficiency. This makes it easier to disagree when it is absolutely necessary.

2. Be willing to concede that sometimes you may be wrong. Don't try constantly to prove that you are better or brighter.

3. Don't ask your colleagues to side with you against the boss – ultimately they may sacrifice you for their own advancement.

4. If you think you are being bullied or harassed, document details of exactly what was said and done where and when, and send a memo to the boss outlining why

you think the behaviour inappropriate. If you don't feel comfortable talking directly to your boss, or you try this and are unsuccessful, reach out to your HR department or another senior manager.

5. If matters are not resolved, update your CV and consider looking for another job. If the harassment is serious, you could pursue redress through industrial tribunals, though there are costs and risks to inform yourself about before pursuing this line of action.

Further Reading

Philip Houston, Michael Floyd and Susan Carnicero, *Get the Truth: Former CIA Officers Teach You How to Persuade Anyone to Tell All*, London: Icon, 2015

Philip Houston, Michael Floyd and Susan Carnicero, *Spy the Lie: Former CIA Officers Teach You How to Detect Deception*, London: Icon, 2012

Glenn Wilson and Chris McLaughlin, *Winning With Body Language*, London: Bloomsbury, 1996

Glenn Wilson, *Psychology for Performing Artists* (2nd edition), London: Whurr, 2002

Index

Other titles in
the Practical Guide series

A Practical Guide to Assertiveness

ISBN: 9781785783319
eISBN: 9781848315228

A Practical Guide to CBT

ISBN: 9781785783845
eISBN: 9781848313231

***A Practical Guide to
CBT for Work***

ISBN: 9781785783333
eISBN: 9781848314351

***A Practical Guide to
Child Psychology***

ISBN: 9781785783227
eISBN: 9781848313293

**A Practical Guide to
Confident Speaking**

ISBN: 9781785783807
eISBN: 9781848316805

**A Practical Guide to
Emotional Intelligence**

ISBN: 9781785783234
eISBN: 9781848314382

***A Practical Guide to
Entrepreneurship***

ISBN: 9781785783814
eISBN: 9781848316270

***A Practical Guide to
Ethics for Everyday Life***

ISBN: 9781785783302
eISBN: 9781848313712

**A Practical Guide to
Happiness**

ISBN: 9781785783241
eISBN: 9781848313637

**A Practical Guide to
Leadership**

ISBN: 9781785783296
eISBN: 9781848315280

A Practical Guide to Management

ISBN: 9781785783784
eISBN: 9781848314252

A Practical Guide to Mindfulness

ISBN: 9781785783838
eISBN: 9781848313750

A Practical Guide to NLP

ISBN: 9781785783906
eISBN: 9781848313255

A Practical Guide to NLP for Work

ISBN: 9781785783265
eISBN: 9781848313811

A Practical Guide to
Philosophy for Everyday Life

ISBN: 9781785783258
eISBN: 9781848313576

A Practical Guide to
Positive Psychology

ISBN: 9781785783852
eISBN: 9781848313736

A Practical Guide to Productivity

ISBN: 9781785783326
eISBN: 9781848316973

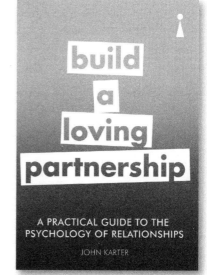

A Practical Guide to the Psychology of Relationships

ISBN: 9781785783289
eISBN: 9781848313606

**A Practical Guide to
Sport Psychology**

ISBN: 9781785783272
eISBN: 9781848313279

**A Practical Guide to the
Psychology of Success**

ISBN: 9781785783890
eISBN: 9781848313316

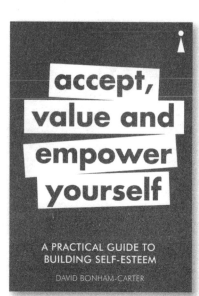

A Practical Guide to Building Self-Esteem

ISBN: 9781785783913
eISBN: 9781848313668

accept,
value and
empower
yourself

A PRACTICAL GUIDE TO
BUILDING SELF-ESTEEM

DAVID BONHAM-CARTER

live well
and
stress-free

A PRACTICAL GUIDE TO
WELL-BEING

PATRICIA FURNESS-SMITH

A Practical Guide to Well-being

ISBN: 9781785783791
eISBN: 9781848318618